Sunset

Southwest
COOK BOOK

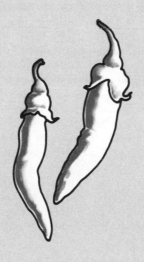

BY THE EDITORS OF SUNSET BOOKS
AND SUNSET MAGAZINE

LANE PUBLISHING CO. • MENLO PARK, CALIFORNIA

RESEARCH & TEXT
JOAN GRIFFITHS
MARY JANE SWANSON

COORDINATING EDITOR
DEBORAH THOMAS KRAMER

DESIGN
CYNTHIA HANSON

ILLUSTRATIONS
SUSAN JAEKEL

PHOTO STYLIST
JOANN MASAOKA

PHOTOGRAPHERS: Tom Wyatt (all except pages 67 and 78); Norman A. Plate (page 78); Darrow M. Watt (page 67).

COVER: The colors of the Southwest are captured in a meal that combines Fajitas, a grilled beef mixture wrapped in a tortilla (page 45), with grilled fresh vegetables, Black Beans (page 69), cilantro-accented Salsa Fresca (page 40), and icy cold Fruited Sangria Punch (page 84). Photography by Tom Wyatt. Photo styling by JoAnn Masaoka. Food styling by Mary Jane Swanson.

A SPIRITED CUISINE

The American Southwest has been the setting for a rich historical pageant—and one happy result is a lively style of cooking which reflects the region's colorful traditions. Now you can re-create the flavor of the Southwest in your own kitchen, with this book as your guide.

You'll learn the secrets fine Southwestern cooks have inherited over the centuries from the Indians, Mexicans, and Spanish. You'll discover, too, innovative uses of traditional seasonings and ingredients, demonstrating the continually evolving character of this vibrant cuisine.

We start off with a primer on the special ingredients that make Southwestern cooking unique, from chiles to cactus leaves to the corn dough—*masa*—used to make tortillas. Then we present a collection of recipes for every course of a Southwestern-style meal, from zesty appetizers to satisfyingly sweet desserts. Choices include the heartiest of traditional fare as well as lighter, more modern interpretations. Alternatives are given for ingredients which may be difficult to find in some locales, so that every cook can create dishes faithful to the spirit of the Southwest.

For our recipes, we provide a nutritional analysis prepared by Hill Nutrition Associates, Inc., of New York, stating calorie count; grams of protein, carbohydrates, and total fat; and milligrams of cholesterol and sodium. Generally, the nutritional information applies to a single serving, based on the largest number of servings given for each recipe.

The nutritional analysis does not include optional ingredients or those for which no specific amount is stated. If an ingredient is listed with an option, the information was calculated using the first choice. Likewise, if a range is given for the amount of an ingredient, values were figured based on the first, lower amount.

We extend special thanks to Rebecca LaBrum and Jane Parkinson for carefully editing the manuscript. For their generosity in sharing props for use in our photographs, we thank Jackie Blank, Crate & Barrel, Tillie Robinett, and Cynthia Scheer.

All of the recipes in this book were tested and developed in the *Sunset* test kitchens.
Sunset Magazine's test kitchens are under the supervision of Jerry Anne Di Vecchio, Home Economics Editor, *Sunset* Magazine.

Sunset Books
   Editor: David E. Clark
   Managing Editor: Elizabeth L. Hogan

First printing October 1987

CONTENTS

This trio of soups—Albuquerque Corn
Soup, Garden Gazpacho, and Chilled
Avocado Soup (recipes on page 13)—
offers lively first-course fare.

SPECIAL FEATURES

A Taste of the Southwest

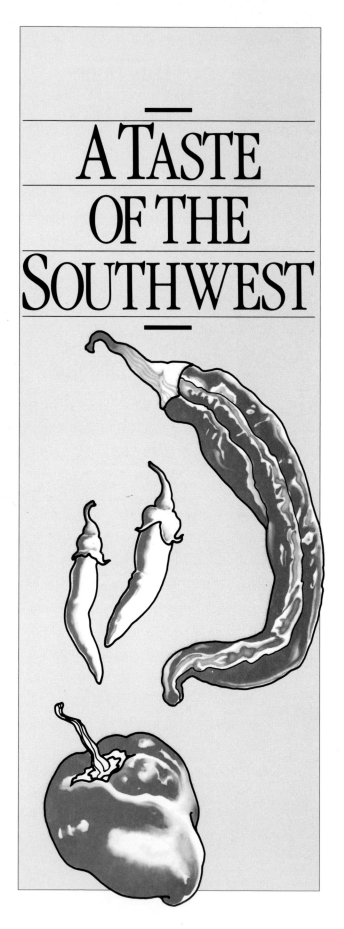

Southwestern cooking is an earthy, richly flavored cuisine, deeply rooted in regional traditions. It is a style based on foods reflecting the colors of South-western terrain: yellow and blue corn, green cactus, brown pinto beans, and brick-red chiles. Indigenous ingredients like these come together in lively crea-tions such as chili con carne, green corn tamales, blue corn tortillas, and barbecued beef ribs—dishes blending native Indian, Spanish, Mexican, and Anglo-American culinary traditions.

For ten centuries, Southwestern Indians, including the Apache, Hopi, Navajo, Papago, Rio Grande Pueblo, and Zuni, lived simply on what the land provided: corn, squash, wild greens, nuts, berries, game, and fish from nearby rivers and streams. But the Indians' simple lifestyle changed when Spanish missionaries came north from Mexico in the 1500s, bringing Mexi-can Indians and their staples: chiles, onions, garlic, tomatoes, avocados, and chocolate. The missionaries also brought favorite foods from their European homeland—wheat, rice, orchard fruits, and grapes.

The cooking styles of the Indians, Spanish, and Mexicans melded over the next three centuries. But after the Mexican War ended in 1848, a new group, the Anglo-American cowboys, settled in the area, bringing herds of cattle to take advantage of the Southwest's extensive grazing land. The new abun-dance of meat inspired beef recipes adapted to the cowboys' life "out on the range"—slow-cooked stews and chilis, and barbecue recipes.

Like all American regional cuisines, today's South-western cooking is influenced by the modern trend toward serving foods that are lower in calories, more nutritious, and more attractively presented. With a wealth of fresh produce at hand, Southwestern cooks have found it easy to show off their native dishes in a lighter, more visually appealing style.

In *Sunset*'s *Southwest Cook Book,* we explore modern Southwestern cuisine in dishes of every kind, from appetizers to desserts. Many of these reci-pes are steeped in tradition, such as Indian Fry Bread, Rio Grande Chili, New Mexican Beef Brisket, and Indian Bean & Lamb Stew. But you'll also find dishes using traditional ingredients in fresh new ways: Spinach Salad with Crisp Red Chiles, Cheese-stuffed Blossom Appetizers, Turkey with Chocolate Orange Sauce, Game Hens with Jalapeño Jelly Glaze, and refreshing ices flavored with pumpkin or pecans. Accompanying each recipe are estimated times for preparation and cooking, and detailed nutritional information.

Along with the recipes, we've included a few special features: an array of Southwestern menus you might serve, a primer on barbecuing techniques, and a selection of lively sauces and salsas.

To help you get started, we begin the book with a glossary of chiles and other ingredients that might be unfamiliar to you.

CHILES

Chiles are the heart, soul, and fire of Southwestern cooking. Regional cooks use them in abundance to give their dishes a rich flavor that varies from mildly spicy to fiery hot, depending on the type of chile used.

Chiles came to the Southwest from Mexico, where more than 140 varieties are grown. On these pages, we discuss the fresh and dried chiles popular in the Southwest and used in our book; we also tell you how to select and handle chiles, how to roast and peel them, and how to make your own ground chile.

Throughout this book, we spell "chile" with a final *e* when referring to the pepper. "Chili" is the spelling used for chili powder—a mixture of dried ground chiles, cumin, oregano, and other seasonings—and for the famous stewlike dish from Texas.

When selecting fresh chiles from the produce section of your market, make sure they are firm, smooth, and glossy, with no splits or signs of withering. To keep them fresh at home, refrigerate them in a plastic bag for up to 3 days.

Chile heat is concentrated in the interior veins near the seed heart—not in the seeds themselves, as is commonly believed. Though there's no sure way to predict how hot a fresh chile will be, smaller types usually pack the biggest punch. But heat levels may vary even within the same variety, depending on the climate and soil where the chiles were grown.

When handling fresh chiles, it's best to protect your hands with rubber gloves and avoid touching your face or eyes. Thoroughly wash any skin area that comes into contact with chile oil.

To roast and peel fresh chiles for chiles rellenos and other dishes, you need to blister the waxy outer skin. There are three ways to do this. First, if you have a gas range, you can rotate the chiles, one at a time, over the flame until they are charred and blistered (1 to 1½ minutes). Second, you can arrange the chiles on a baking sheet, set them 3 inches below a preheated broiler unit, and broil them until blistered (6 to 8 minutes), turning frequently. Finally, to peel a large number of chiles, arrange them slightly apart on baking sheets and roast, uncovered, in a 450° oven, turning several times, until the skin is brown and blistered (about 20 to 30 minutes).

After blistering chiles by any technique, place them in a plastic bag while still warm; twist bag to close, then let chiles sweat until they're cool enough to handle. Peel off the skins, then remove and discard the stems and seeds. Use chiles or refrigerate for up to 3 days.

Dried chiles of several varieties are even more important in Southwestern cuisine than fresh ones, probably because they're always available. Look for dried chiles near the spices in Mexican grocery stores, or in the Mexican products section or fresh produce section of a well-stocked market. Usually sold in cellophane bags, dried chiles should look pliable and not cracked or overdry. If powder is evident in the bag, the chiles may be old.

Making your own ground chile (true chile powder) from whole dried chiles is easy, but it can be messy. The first step is to roast the dried chiles on a baking sheet in a 350° oven until very dry and crisp (5 to 10 minutes), turning once or twice. When chiles are cool enough to handle, break them into pieces, discarding stems and seeds. Grind chile pieces into a fine powder in a blender or coffee grinder. Store the powder in a glass jar in a cool, dark place. Be sure to label the powder with the type of dried chile you used. Ground chile may also be purchased at markets that stock Mexican products.

CHILE VARIETIES

Much disagreement and confusion surrounds chile nomenclature. Several different names can apply to one kind of chile; a single chile may have different names in its fresh and dried forms. We hope the following descriptions help clear up a little of the confusion.

■ **ANAHEIM** (also called California, New Mexico, or Rio Grande green chile). This pointed, 6- to 7-inch-long chile is bright green, turning to red as it ripens. Probably the most popular and widely available fresh chile in the United States, the Anaheim has a mild to medium-hot flavor. Many are processed and sold as canned green chiles. Dried Anaheims are usually labeled California or New Mexico dried chiles.

■ **ANCHO** (also called poblano and, mistakenly, pasilla chile; see also Pasilla, page 7). This large, triangular chile is the dried form of the fresh poblano chile. It is most commonly used for making *mole* sauces. Dried anchos are sometimes labeled pasilla chiles; this is the name commonly given the chile in Baja California, where much of the crop is grown.

■ **CALIFORNIA** (also called Anaheim). Dried Anaheims are usually labeled California dried chiles. Like New Mexico dried chiles (see page 7), they are typically soaked in hot liquid and puréed for use in cooking.

■ **CASCABEL.** A pungent, round Mexican chile, usually sold dried in Mexican stores. When this chile is shaken, its seeds rattle—hence the name *cascabel,* which means "jingle bells" in Spanish.

■ **CAYENNE.** These 2- to 3-inch-long, thin, fiery hot chiles are usually dried, then sold whole or ground into a powder. The canned commercial powder is often a mixture of hot dried chiles, and hence, labeled simply ground red pepper.

Serrano

Chile de Arbol

Jalapeño

Dried Guajillo

Anaheim

Dried
New Mexico

Thai

Poblano

Santa Fe
Grande

■ **CHILE DE ARBOL**. This small hot chile is similar to the cayenne chile; see page 5.

■ **CHIPOTLE**. Chipotle is not a chile variety, but the name given to smoked and dried jalapeños. Though you can sometimes find whole dried chipotle chiles in Mexican stores, they're more typically sold canned in *adobo* or *adobado* sauce (a tomato-based sauce) or *en escabeche* (a pickling mixture).

■ **FRESNO** (sometimes called hot chile in the Southwest or, mistakenly, Santa Fe Grande). Like Anaheims, these bright green chiles turn red when ripe. They're named after the place where they were first grown—Fresno, California. Fresno chiles are shaped very much like jalapeños and are often confused with them, but their flavor is slightly milder. Nonetheless, they make a good substitute for jalapeños.

■ **GUAJILLO** (also called Mirasol). A dried brownish-orange chile frequently sold in Mexican markets, the Guajillo has a distinctive fruity-hot flavor. Fresh Guajillos are more commonly called Mirasol chiles.

■ **GÜERO** (sometimes confused with jalapeño or Santa Fe Grande chile). *Güero* means "blond" in Spanish—and the güero chile is pale yellow to yellow-green, ripening to dark red. This 1- to 5-inch-long chile is usually hot to fiery, and can be substituted for jalapeños, serranos, or Santa Fe Grande chiles.

■ **JALAPEÑO**. Originally from Jalapa in the state of Veracruz, Mexico, the jalapeño is a favorite hot chile in the Southwest and West. Look for these bright green, 2½- to 3½-inch-long chiles fresh in the produce sections of most markets, or buy them pickled. They can substitute for most hot chiles. Smoked and dried jalapeños are called chipotle chiles.

■ **MIRASOL**. *See* Guajillo, above.

■ **MULATO** (sometimes confused with fresh poblano or dried ancho). This dark green, fleshy chile looks like a large fresh poblano and has the same mild to medium-hot flavor. Fresh, it can be used for chiles rellenos. Dried mulatos have a dark chocolate-brown color; in Mexico, they're frequently made into a paste and sold for use in *mole* sauces.

■ **NEW MEXICO** (sometimes called California or Anaheim chile). These mild to medium-hot chiles, very much like Anaheims in flavor, are often seen strung into ropes or *ristras* and hung to dry outside Southwestern homes. The fresh chiles turn from green to scarlet as they ripen; they make excellent chiles rellenos. But it's the dried version (interchangeable with California dried chiles) that's most typically used in Southwestern cooking. The dried chiles are usually soaked in hot liquid for 30 minutes, then puréed and added to chilis, stews, and many sauces. Dried New Mexico chiles may also be ground to a powder and sold as ground New Mexico chile.

■ **PASILLA** (mistakenly called poblano or ancho chile; labeled *chile negro* or black chile when dried). There is much confusion over the name of this mild to medium-hot chile. Poblano chiles are often sold under the name pasilla, but true pasillas don't really resemble poblanos. The pasilla is a thin, 5- to 7-inch-long chile, chocolate brown when fresh and ripe, black when dried. Most pasillas are sold in dried form; their flavor makes them a good substitute for anchos.

■ **PEQUIN** (or Chilipiquin). These tiny, round to oval, fiery hot chiles are primarily used for commercial liquid hot pepper sauce. They're sold dried in Mexican markets, and may be substituted for cayenne chiles.

■ **POBLANO** (also called ancho and, mistakenly, pasilla). Very dark green and triangular in shape, the poblano chile measures 3 to 5 inches long and 2 to 3 inches wide at the stem end. It's often confused with the fresh pasilla chile. The poblano's mild to medium-hot flavor makes it well suited for chiles rellenos. Dried poblanos are called anchos.

■ **SANDIA**. This tapering, 5- to 7-inch-long chile is a hybrid of the Anaheim chile, and can be used interchangeably in cooking with Anaheim, California, or New Mexico chiles. But unlike these, it's typically sold fresh and *ripe*—when it's bright red. In the Southwest, it's sometimes used to make jelly.

■ **SANTA FE GRANDE**. These chiles are like Fresnos in heat level and size—but while Fresnos turn red as they ripen, Santa Fes take on a yellow hue. Santa Fe and Fresno chiles are interchangeable in cooking.

■ **SERRANO**. This popular medium bright green to dark green chile resembles a small jalapeño, but its flavor is slightly hotter. It's usually sold fresh or pickled; fresh serranos are used in salsas and sauces, while the pickled chiles add a lively accent to sandwiches and salads. Serranos can be used as a substitute for jalapeños, Fresnos, or Santa Fe Grandes.

■ **TEPIN** (or Chiltecpin). Small (just ¼ inch in diameter) and very hot, tepin chiles are sometimes found dried in Mexican markets. They can be substituted for pequin or cayenne chiles.

■ **THAI**. A label sometimes posted on tiny hot red and green chiles used in Southeast Asian cooking, Thai chiles are becoming increasingly available in the Southwest and West. They're sold in the produce section of well-stocked markets.

OTHER INGREDIENTS

■ **ACHIOTE**. Brick-red achiote seeds come from the tropical annatto tree, first brought to the Southwest from Mexico's Yucatán peninsula. Before use, the seeds must be soaked overnight in water, then puréed to make a paste. Like paprika, achiote adds a subtle,

(Continued on page 10)

Southwest Menu Ideas

Menus featuring Southwestern recipes can be as elegant as a sit-down dinner of barbecued duck with chile-orange sauce or as casual as a beach picnic of spicy chili and cornbread. But they always include foods that are festive and full-flavored.

To get you started entertaining Southwest style, we've assembled menus for twelve different occasions. Some serve small groups of four or six; others are geared for larger gatherings. All our menus include at least three recipes from this book.

An Adjustable-size Breakfast

Whether you're serving two or twelve for breakfast, these omelets will fit the occasion. Accompany the festive entrée with sopaipillas and mugs of spicy chocolate. Quantities can be adjusted to suit the number of guests.

Red Chile & Cheese Omelet (page 65)
Sopaipillas (page 82)   Butter   Honey
Cantaloupe Wedges
New Mexican Hot Chocolate (page 84)

A Very Southwestern Brunch

South-of-the-border flavors are evident in much of Southwestern cuisine, as exemplified in this special brunch menu for six. To save time, make the Black Beans and the sauces for the Huevos Rancheros a day ahead. Double the recipe for Sangrita so there is plenty for guests to sip on arrival.

Tomato-Orange Sangrita (page 84)
Huevos Rancheros (page 66)
Black Beans (page 69)
Warm Corn Tortillas   Butter
Pineapple Spears

A Cool Summer Luncheon

Spicy-hot and refreshingly cool flavors complement each other in the entrée for this hot weather luncheon for six. For carefree serving, prepare the salad, bread, and dessert a day ahead.

Chile, Shrimp & Corn Salad (page 64)
Green Chile Bread (page 85)   Butter
Papaya Wedges with Lime
Vanilla Ice Cream   Piñon Fingers (page 92)

A Finger Food Feast for Four

Several favorite Southwestern foods—native quail, fresh corn tamales, and dried fruit pastries called *pastelitos*—are combined in this finger-food menu.

Crisp Raw Vegetables
Quail with Chipotle Chiles (page 60)
Green Corn Tamales (page 33)
Pastelitos (page 92)

A Condiment Soup Party

Planning a party, even for two dozen guests, is easy when the main course is a make-ahead soup that guests can serve and embellish themselves. To complete the menu for 24, make double recipes of the punch, the cheese crisps, and the mango dessert.

Fruited Sangria Punch (page 84)
Arizona Cheese Crisps (page 18)
Black Bean Soup (page 26)
Sheepherder's Bread (page 82)   Butter
Mango Cream (page 93)
Bizcochitos (page 90)

COOL WEATHER PICNIC FOR SIX

To keep you warm on those cool days at the beach or park, we suggest this easy-to-tote ground beef chili served with squares of moist Mexican-style cornbread.

Guacamole (page 16) with Vegetable Dippers
New Mexican Red Bean Chili (page 23)
Mexicana Cornbread (page 80)
Grapes   Buñuelos (page 89)

A RIB-STICKING BARBECUE

Ever since the days when Indians roasted foods over an open fire, barbecuing has been a favorite method of cooking in the Southwest. In this menu for six, short ribs take advantage of a more modern technique —cooking on a covered barbecue.

Offer small salad servings or double the recipe, depending on appetites.

Garden Gazpacho (page 13)
Barbecued Beef Short Ribs (page 45)
Corn on the Cob
Asparagus with Tomatillos (page 74)
Buñuelos (page 89)
Ice Cream

TEXAS-STYLE BARBECUE BUFFET

Slowly simmered in a sauce of New Mexican red chiles, this beef brisket makes an easy but very flavorful main dish. To complete the menu for 12, make double recipes of the salad and the bread pudding and a triple recipe of the chiles.

Romaine & Cactus Salad (page 15)
New Mexican Beef Brisket (page 47)
Roasted Cheese-stuffed Chiles (page 71)
Las Cruces Bread Pudding (page 92)

A FRESH FISH CELEBRATION

If you're lucky enough to catch a red snapper or other firm-textured white fish, try presenting it whole, baked in a cinnamon-spiked tomato sauce. Accompany the spicy entrée for six with cool coleslaw with cilantro.

Tex-Mex Red Snapper (page 63)
Red Bell Pepper Pasta (page 73)
or Steamed Rice
Cilantro Slaw (page 74)
Baked Apples with Cowboy Cream (page 93)

THANKSGIVING FIESTA FOR A DOZEN

Spanish-Mexican flavors liven up this Thanksgiving dinner. Double recipes of the bean dip, salsa, tamales, and flan can be prepared a day before the celebration.

Antojitos Tray (page 16)
Black Bean Appetizer (page 17)
Grilled Turkey, Southwest Style (page 61)
Cranberry Salsa (page 40)
Grilled Zucchini & Red Onion Halves
Small Cheese Tamales (page 33)
Sweet Potatoes with Tequila & Lime (page 69)
Spiced Caramel Custard Flan (page 89)

AN ELEGANT SIT-DOWN DINNER

A tart, spicy-hot orange sauce dresses up this brace of ducks in an elegant menu designed to serve six. Cooking the birds on the barbecue not only gives them a smoky flavor, but simplifies kitchen cleanup.

Duck with Citrus-Chile Marinade (page 60)
Baked Winter Squash
Blue Corn Muffins (page 79)
Orange & Avocado Salad with Cumin Vinaigrette (page 72)
Creamy Pecan or Pumpkin Ice (page 90)

A LATE EVENING REPAST

Just three dishes—chimichangas, salad, and dessert— add up to an unusually festive post-opera or movie menu for four.

Oven-fried Chimichangas (page 36)
Marinated Bell Pepper Strips (page 74)
Sour Cream–topped Pineapple (page 93)

...Continued from page 7

earthy flavor and lots of red color to fish and poultry dishes. Look for achiote seeds near the other seasonings in Mexican markets.

■ **ATOLE.** *See* Blue corn.

■ **BLUE CORN.** A crop native to New Mexico, blue corn has a distinctive color and an earthy flavor. It's usually dried and ground into meal (or flour) for making tortillas and baked goods. Blue cornmeal is becoming increasingly available outside New Mexico, and is sold by a number of health food and specialty food stores in the Southwest and West. Look for the meal in two grinds: *harina para tortillas,* a coarse grind, and *harina para atole,* a fine grind. (Before purchasing, check your recipe to see which type you need.)

If you can't find blue cornmeal in your area, you can order it by mail from the following three sources in New Mexico: Blue Corn Connection, 8812 Fourth St. N.W., Albuquerque 87114, (505) 897-2412; Casados Farms, Box 852, San Juan Pueblo 87566, (505) 852-2433; Josie's Best Mexican Foods, Box 5525, Santa Fe 87502, (505) 983-6520.

■ **CHAYOTE.** A tropical summer squash that was grown centuries ago by the Aztec and Mayan Indians of Mexico, the chayote is a pale green, pear-shaped vegetable with deeply furrowed skin. To prepare it, simply rinse well; then slice thinly through the seed (it's edible). Steam or boil as for zucchini.

■ **CHEESE.** Several Mexican cheeses, primarily produced in California, are commonly used in Southwest cooking. *Queso fresco,* or fresh cheese (also called *ranchero*), is the most widely distributed. Its lumpy texture and mild flavor make it similar to farmers cheese. *Asadero* is a buttery-flavored string cheese that is stretched and rolled into balls, or shaped into logs and sold in tortilla-size slices. It's similar to mozzarella but tangier in flavor. *Cotija* (also called *queso seco* or dry cheese) is a dry, crumbly cheese similar to Parmesan but milder in flavor.

■ **CORN HUSKS.** A necessary ingredient for making tamales, corn husks are usually sold dried in Mexican markets or markets well-stocked with Mexican products.

To soak for tamales, discard bits of dried silk and other extraneous materials. Cover with **warm water** and let stand until pliable (about 2 hours or until next day).

■ **EPAZOTE** (sometimes called wormseed or goosefoot). This medicinal-tasting herb is used in the cuisine of the Yucatán peninsula in Mexico. Though epazote grows easily from seed, it's hard to find fresh in U.S. markets. Look for the dried herb in Mexican markets, or order the seeds from Horticultural Enterprises, Box 810082, Dallas, Texas 75381-0082. There is no substitute for this herb.

■ **JICAMA** (pronounced HEE-kah-mah). A popular Mexican root vegetable, jicama looks like a giant brown turnip. Its thick brown skin conceals crisp, white, slightly sweet flesh that resembles a water chestnut in both texture and flavor. Typically served as an appetizer with lime and salt or other dips, it can be used as a substitute for water chestnuts in Chinese cooking.

■ **HOMINY** (also called *pozole* or *posole*). Hominy is simply large dried white or yellow corn kernels that have been soaked in a lime solution to remove their hulls; it's sold dried, frozen, and canned. The partially cooked frozen product has the best flavor, but it can be found only in some Mexican markets. The dried form is somewhat more available at Mexican markets; canned hominy is readily available in almost all grocery stores.

■ **MASA & MASA HARINA.** *Masa* is the Spanish word for the corn dough used to make tortillas and tamales. It can be purchased already mixed in some Mexican delicatessens or in tortilla factories in the Southwest. *Masa harina,* marketed by the Quaker Oats Company (the name is a registered trademark), is a dehydrated corn flour which can easily be made into masa.

■ **NOPALES** (cactus leaves). These flat, prickly, light green leaves of the prickly pear cactus are sometimes sold fresh in Southwestern and Western markets, but they're more commonly found canned. The fresh leaves must be peeled and blanched before using. Look for fresh nopales in the produce department and canned nopales in the Mexican food section of well-stocked markets.

■ **PEPITAS.** Pepitas are raw, unsalted pumpkin seeds, usually found in health food stores.

■ **PIÑONS** (also called pine nuts or pignolias). Small, oval, cream-colored piñons come from the pine trees growing in the deserts of the Southwest. Since they're hand-gathered, they're expensive, but there's no substitute for the distinctive flavor they add to Southwestern dishes. Piñons are sold in most well-stocked supermarkets; look for them alongside the other packaged nuts.

■ **POZOLE.** *See* Hominy.

■ **PRICKLY PEAR FRUITS.** These bright red fruits of a native Mexican cactus plant have dark, red-purple flesh that is juicy and delicately sweet. They must be peeled (wear rubber gloves) before serving.

■ **TOMATILLOS.** Tomatillos resemble small green tomatoes enclosed in papery husks. Their tart, slightly fruity flavor provides the base for many Southwestern sauces. Both fresh and canned tomatillos are sold in well-stocked markets—the fresh fruit in the produce section, the canned type in the Mexican food section.

A Southwest Thanksgiving serves up traditional foods with a spicy twist. Accompany Grilled Turkey, Southwest Style (page 61) with grilled zucchini and red onions, Small Cheese Tamales (page 33), Sweet Potatoes with Tequila & Lime (page 69), and Cranberry Salsa (page 40).

MEAL OPENERS

LIGHT SOUPS, SALADS & APPETIZERS

—

Whether it's an eat-out-of-hand nibble or a sit-down first course, the meal opener is extremely important in any Southwestern dinner.

Guacamole, seasoned black beans with a spicy salsa, and bubbly grilled cheese embellished with shrimp are established favorites. Crisp-fried Tortilla Pieces (page 77) are the perfect scoopers for these appetizers. Crisp flour tortillas topped with cheese, chiles, and chorizo and served hot from the oven are another popular snack; they're known as Arizona Cheese Crisps.

Light soups, either hot or chilled, can also set the stage for the rest of the meal. Albuquerque Corn Soup, Garden Gazpacho, and Chilled Avocado Soup are three we suggest here.

A cool, crisp salad is the perfect foil for a spicy main course to follow. Tangy tomatillos star in two of the salads in this chapter; tender, mild cactus, either fresh or canned, lends a regional flavor to two others.

CHILLED AVOCADO SOUP

Pictured on page 3

Preparation time: About 25 minutes
Chilling time: At least 4 hours or until next day

While the meat cooks on the grill, offer mugs of this creamy chilled soup and perhaps some salted pumpkin seeds to tickle appetites.

- 1 tablespoon salad oil
- 1 clove garlic, minced or pressed
- ½ cup chopped onion
- 3 large ripe avocados
- ¼ cup lemon juice
- 3 tablespoons dry sherry
- 1 tablespoon chicken-stock base
- 2½ cups hot water
- ¾ teaspoon liquid hot pepper seasoning
- 2 tablespoons chopped fresh cilantro (coriander)
- 2 cups milk
  Salt

Heat oil in a small pan over medium heat. Add garlic and onion; cook, stirring often, until onion is soft (about 10 minutes). Set aside to cool.

Pit and peel 2 of the avocados, then slice into a blender. Add lemon juice, onion mixture, and sherry and whirl until puréed. In a bowl, mix chicken-stock base with hot water until dissolved; add to avocado mixture along with hot pepper seasoning, then whirl until smoothly puréed. Pour purée into a bowl and stir in cilantro and milk. Season to taste with salt. Cover; refrigerate for at least 4 hours or until next day.

Pit, peel, and slice remaining avocado. Ladle soup into mugs; top with avocado. Makes 6 servings.

Per serving: 299 calories, 6 g protein, 16 g carbohydrates, 25 g total fat, 13 mg cholesterol, 268 mg sodium

ALBUQUERQUE CORN SOUP

Pictured on page 3

Preparation time: 20 to 25 minutes

Remember this soup when the "corn is as high as an elephant's eye"—July through September in most areas. It goes well with a main-dish salad.

- ¼ cup butter or margarine
- 3½ cups (5 to 6 ears) corn cut from cob
- 1 clove garlic, minced or pressed

- 1 cup regular-strength chicken broth
- 2 cups milk
- 1 teaspoon dry oregano leaves
- 1 can (4 oz.) diced green chiles
- 1 cup (4 oz.) shredded jack cheese
  Salt
  Fresh cilantro (coriander) or oregano sprigs

Melt butter in a 5- to 6-quart pan over medium heat. Add corn and garlic; cook, stirring, until corn is hot and darker golden (about 2 minutes). Remove from heat. Whirl broth and 2 cups of the corn in a blender until puréed; return to pan. Stir in milk, oregano, and chiles. Bring to a boil, stirring, over medium heat. Remove from heat and stir in cheese. Season to taste with salt. Transfer soup to a serving container; garnish with cilantro. Makes about 6 servings.

Per serving: 276 calories, 11 g protein, 22 g carbohydrates, 17 g total fat, 49 mg cholesterol, 516 mg sodium

GARDEN GAZPACHO

Pictured on page 3

Preparation time: 20 to 25 minutes
Chilling time: 4 hours or until next day

If you like spicy flavors, make this refreshing soup with tomato cocktail; choose broth for a milder, lighter version.

- 1 large cucumber
- 2 large tomatoes, seeded and chopped
- 1 large red or green bell pepper, seeded and chopped
- 1 can (2¼ oz.) sliced ripe olives, drained
- ¼ cup lime juice
- 4 cups regular-strength chicken broth or spicy tomato cocktail
- 1 clove garlic, minced or pressed
- ½ cup sliced green onions (including tops)
- 1 tablespoon minced fresh thyme or 1 teaspoon dry thyme leaves
  Liquid hot pepper seasoning

Peel cucumber and cut in half lengthwise; scrape out and discard seeds. Chop cucumber.

In a large bowl, combine cucumber, tomatoes, bell pepper, olives, lime juice, broth, garlic, onions, and thyme. Season to taste with hot pepper seasoning. Cover; refrigerate for at least 4 hours or until next day. To serve, ladle into mugs. Makes 6 to 8 servings.

Per serving: 47 calories, 2 g protein, 4 g carbohydrates, 2 g total fat, 0 mg cholesterol, 568 mg sodium

Dried chile strips crisped in oil accent the nippy greens, red onion, cactus, and avocados in
our Spinach Salad with Crisp Red Chiles (recipe on facing page).
When cool, the red-hued chile oil becomes the base for a tangy dressing.

Spinach Salad with Crisp Red Chiles

Pictured on facing page

Preparation time: 40 to 50 minutes if using fresh cactus; 25 to 30 if using canned nopalitos
Chilling time: At least 30 minutes to crisp greens

The bold flavor and color of red chiles provide contrast to cool cactus and crisp spinach. Look for cactus, fresh or canned, in Mexican markets.

- 1 **pound spinach**
- ¼ **pound watercress**
- 6 **large dried red New Mexico or California chiles**
- ¼ **cup olive oil or salad oil**
- 1 **pound fresh whole or diced cactus (*nopales*) or 1 jar (15 oz.) *nopalitos*, drained and rinsed**
- 1 **large red onion, thinly sliced**
- 1 **cup sliced radishes**
- 1 **pound *asadero* (Mexican-style string cheese) or mozzarella cheese, cut into ½-inch cubes**
  Cider Dressing (recipe follows)
- 2 **large ripe avocados**

Discard tough spinach and watercress stems; wash greens separately and pat dry. Wrap in paper towels, enclose in plastic bags, and refrigerate for at least 30 minutes or up to 2 days.

With scissors, cut chiles crosswise into thin strips; discard seeds and stems. In a wide frying pan over low heat, stir oil and chiles until chiles are crisp (2 to 3 minutes). Watch closely to avoid burning. Lift chiles from oil; set aside. Save oil for dressing.

To prepare fresh cactus: If whole cactus pad has thorns or prickly hairs, hold pad with tongs and use a knife to scrape off thorns or hairs (wear gloves). Trim around edge of pad to remove skin and any thorns, then peel remaining pad if skin is tough. Cut into about ½-inch squares.

In a 3- to 4-quart pan over high heat, bring 8 cups water to a boil. Add fresh cactus, reduce heat, and simmer, uncovered, until cactus is barely tender when pierced (about 5 minutes). Drain, rinse well, and drain again. (If using canned cactus, omit cooking.)

Tear spinach into bite-size pieces; you should have 3 to 4 quarts. Place half the spinach in a large salad bowl. Top with half each of the watercress, onion, radishes, cactus, and cheese. Repeat layers. (At this point, you may cover and refrigerate for up to 4 hours.)

To serve, prepare Cider Dressing. Pit, peel, and slice avocados; add to salad with chiles. Spoon dressing over salad; toss. Makes 6 to 8 servings.

Cider Dressing. Mix **oil from chiles**; ⅔ cup **cider vinegar**; 1 clove **garlic**, minced or pressed; 1 tablespoon **soy sauce**; and ¼ teaspoon **pepper.**

Per serving: 375 calories, 15 g protein, 17 g carbohydrates, 30 g total fat, 44 mg cholesterol, 390 mg sodium

Romaine & Cactus Salad

Preparation time: 35 to 45 minutes if using fresh cactus; 20 to 25 minutes if using canned nopalitos
Chilling time: At least 30 minutes

If you use fresh cactus, prepare it as directed for Spinach Salad with Crisp Red Chiles (at left). Tender and mild, the pads taste something like cucumber.

- 3 **quarts water**
- 2 **large onions, sliced**
- 1 **pound fresh whole or diced cactus (*nopales*) or 1 jar (15 oz.) *nopalitos*, drained and rinsed**
- 1 **pound romaine lettuce**
  Cilantro Dressing (recipe follows)
- 1 **cup (about 4 oz.) coarsely grated *cotija* (Mexican-style dry white cheese) or 1 cup (about 5 oz.) grated Parmesan cheese**
- 2 **large tomatoes, cut into wedges**
- ½ **cup large pitted ripe olives**

Bring water to boiling in a 5- to 6-quart pan over high heat. Add onions and cook until slightly wilted (1 to 2 minutes). Lift out with a slotted spoon; drain and set aside. Add diced fresh cactus to boiling water and cook until barely tender when pierced (about 5 minutes). Drain, rinse well, and drain again. When onions and cactus are cool, separately cover and refrigerate for at least 30 minutes or until next day. (If using canned cactus, omit cooking; simply chill as directed.)

Wash lettuce and pat dry; refrigerate for at least 30 minutes or until next day. Meanwhile, prepare Cilantro Dressing.

On a large platter or 6 plates, arrange romaine leaves. Place a band of cooked onions over romaine, then top with cactus and cheese. Garnish with tomatoes and olives. Drizzle with Cilantro Dressing. Makes 6 servings.

Cilantro Dressing. Mix ½ cup **salad oil**; ¼ cup **lime juice**; 1 clove **garlic**, minced or pressed; and ⅓ cup chopped **fresh cilantro** (coriander).

Per serving: 344 calories, 13 g protein, 12 g carbohydrates, 28 g total fat, 19 mg cholesterol, 537 mg sodium

Tomatillo, Jicama & Apple Salad

Preparation time: 20 to 25 minutes

A refreshing, low-calorie combination, this salad can be picked up to eat as an appetizer or served with the main course.

> 2 **tart, green-skinned apples**
>   **About 2 tablespoons lime juice**
>   **About 1 pound jicama**
> 8 **tomatillos,** *each* **about 1½-inch-diameter**
>   **Fresh cilantro (coriander) leaves**
>   **Coarse salt**

Core apples and cut each into 16 thin wedges. Coat with lime juice. Scrub and peel jicama, then cut into 32 thin wedges. Husk and wash tomatillos; cut into 32 slices.

On each slice of jicama, stack 1 apple slice, 1 tomatillo slice, and a cilantro leaf. Arrange on a platter. Serve, or cover and refrigerate for up to 2 hours. Sprinkle with remaining lime juice and salt. Makes 8 to 10 servings.

Per serving: 47 calories, 1 g protein, 10 g carbohydrates, .44 g total fat, 0 mg cholesterol, 3 mg sodium

Tomatillo & Cheese Salad

Preparation time: About 10 minutes

Tomatillos look like green tomatoes but have a lime-like tartness and a tender-crisp texture. When you buy them, look for smooth fruit that's firm to the touch.

> 1   **pound tomatillos**
> ¼   **cup olive oil**
> 2   **tablespoons lime juice**
> 1   **cup (about 5 oz.) grated Parmesan cheese**
>   **Pepper**

Husk and wash tomatillos. Slice thinly and arrange on a platter or 4 salad plates. Combine oil and lime juice; sprinkle over tomatillos, then sprinkle evenly with cheese. Season to taste with pepper. Makes 4 servings.

Per serving: 311 calories, 16 g protein, 7 g carbohydrates, 25 g total fat, 28 mg cholesterol, 661 mg sodium

Antojitos Tray

Preparation time: 20 to 30 minutes

You can assemble this fresh fruit and vegetable tray a day ahead, then cover and refrigerate until serving time.

> 3   **large oranges**
> 1   **medium-size pineapple (about 3 lbs.)**
> 1½ **pounds jicama**
>   **About ½ cup lime juice**
> ¼   **cup salt**
> 1   **tablespoon paprika**
> 1   **teaspoon ground red pepper (cayenne) or chili powder**
>   **Lime wedges**

Cut each unpeeled orange into 8 wedges. Cut unpeeled pineapple crosswise into ½-inch-thick slices, remove core, and cut each slice into quarters. Scrub and peel jicama; cut into ¼- by ¼- by 3-inch sticks. Coat fruit and jicama with lime juice, then arrange on a serving tray.

Mix salt, paprika, and red pepper in a small serving bowl; place in center of tray and accompany with lime wedges.

To eat, squeeze lime over foods and dip into salt mixture. Makes 10 to 16 servings.

Per serving: 62 calories, 1 g protein, 17 g carbohydrates, .46 g total fat, 0 mg cholesterol, 828 mg sodium

Guacamole

Preparation time: About 15 minutes

This longtime favorite dip is extremely versatile. It can also be used as a sauce for meats and main dishes, or as a dressing for salads.

> 2   **large ripe avocados**
> 2   **to 3 tablespoons lemon or lime juice**
> 1   **clove garlic, minced or pressed**
> 1   **to 2 tablespoons chopped fresh cilantro (coriander)**
> 2   **to 4 canned green chiles, rinsed, seeded, and chopped**
> 1   **medium-size tomato, peeled, seeded, and chopped**
>   **Minced jalapeño or serrano chiles (optional)**
>   **Salt**

Fresh cilantro (coriander) sprigs
Crisp-fried Tortilla Pieces (page 77) or purchased tortilla chips

Cut avocados in half, remove pits, and scoop out pulp. Mash pulp coarsely with a fork; blend in lemon juice, garlic, chopped cilantro, green chiles, tomato, and jalapeño chiles to taste, if used. Season to taste with salt. Spoon into a serving bowl and garnish with cilantro sprigs. Serve with Crisp-fried Tortilla Pieces. Makes about 1⅔ cups.

Per tablespoon: 34 calories, .49 g protein, 2 g carbohydrates, 3 g total fat, 0 mg cholesterol, 69 mg sodium

GRILLED CHEESE DIP

Preparation time: 25 to 30 minutes
Heating time: About 10 minutes

While the chef tends the meat, guests can help themselves to this melted cheese treat at the side of the grill.

- 1½ **tablespoons olive oil**
- 1 **large onion, chopped**
- 2 **large tomatoes, seeded and coarsely chopped**
- ¼ **teaspoon ground cinnamon**
- 7 **to 9 small fresh or canned jalapeño chiles**
  Salt
- 2 **pounds mild cheese, such as jack, Muenster, teleme, fontina, or Gouda**
- 1 **cup small cooked shrimp**
- 10 **to 12 cups Crisp-fried Tortilla Pieces (page 77) or purchased tortilla chips**

Heat oil in a wide frying pan over medium heat. Add onion and cook, stirring often, until soft (about 10 minutes). Add tomatoes and cinnamon. Stir over high heat for 1 minute. Remove from heat. Rinse, seed, and chop 4 to 6 of the chiles; stir into onion mixture. Season to taste with salt. Set aside. If made ahead, let cool; cover and refrigerate until next day.

Trim any wax coating from cheese; cut cheese into ¼-inch-thick slices. Arrange in an 8- to 10-inch metal pan at least 1½ inches deep, overlapping slices to cover pan bottom and extend up just to edges. Spoon tomato mixture over cheese in a 6-inch circle. Top with shrimp and remaining whole chiles.

Place pan on a barbecue grill 4 to 6 inches above a partial bed of medium coals; keep a section of fire grate empty so there's a cool area on grill. Let cheese melt, checking frequently to be sure cheese isn't scorching on bottom. (If cheese is getting hot too fast, move it to cool area of grill.)

To eat, scoop up melted cheese mixture with tortilla pieces. Makes 12 to 16 servings.

Per serving of dip: 250 calories, 17 g protein, 4 g carbohydrates, 19 g total fat, 63 mg cholesterol, 320 mg sodium

BLACK BEAN APPETIZER

Preparation time: 25 to 30 minutes
Cooking time: 2 to 2½ hours

Scoop up puréed black beans and cheese with Crisp-fried Tortilla Pieces, then dip into a spicy-hot salsa for a stick-to-the-ribs appetizer.

- ¼ **pound (about ⅔ cup) dried black beans**
- ¼ **pound salt pork, diced**
- 1 **small onion, chopped**
- 4 **large cloves garlic, minced or pressed**
  About 2 cups water
- ¼ **cup lightly packed fresh cilantro (coriander)**
  Hot Salsa (recipe follows)
- 3 **tablespoons crumbled *cotija* (Mexican-style dry white cheese) or grated Parmesan cheese**
  Crisp-fried Tortilla Pieces (page 77) or purchased tortilla chips
  Fresh cilantro (coriander) sprigs

Sort beans to remove any debris; rinse and set aside. In a 3-quart pan over medium-high heat, cook salt pork until fat is rendered; stir occasionally. Add onion and garlic; stir often until onion is soft (about 10 minutes). Add 2 cups water, beans, and the ¼ cup cilantro. Bring to a boil; reduce heat, cover, and simmer until beans are tender to bite—2 to 2½ hours. (At this point, you may let cool, then cover and refrigerate for up to 4 days. Reheat to continue.)

Meanwhile, prepare Hot Salsa. Set aside. In a food processor or blender, purée bean mixture, adding water if needed to make 1½ cups.

Mound bean mixture in center of a platter; evenly sprinkle with cheese. Arrange tortilla pieces beside beans. Pour salsa into a small bowl; garnish with cilantro. To eat, scoop tortilla pieces through beans and then through salsa. Makes 6 servings.

Per serving: 223 calories, 6 g protein, 13 g carbohydrates, 16 g total fat, 18 mg cholesterol, 321 mg sodium

HOT SALSA. Mix ¼ cup **lime juice** with 2 tablespoons finely chopped **small fresh hot chiles** (such as jalapeño or Fresno) and 1 tablespoon chopped **fresh cilantro** (coriander), optional.

Per tablespoon: 3 calories, .08 g protein, 1 g carbohydrates, .02 g total fat, 0 mg cholesterol, 2 mg sodium

Arizona Cheese Crisps

Pictured on facing page

Preparation time: 10 to 15 minutes (allow an additional 30 minutes if you make your own tortillas)
Cooking time: About 5 minutes to fry each tortilla; 7 minutes to bake

A hot, crackly concoction, cheese crisps look much like a thin pizza with bent sides. Simply break off chunks to eat out of hand.

> **Lard or salad oil**
>
> 6 **flour tortillas (10-inch-diameter),**
> **4 flour tortillas (12-inch-diameter), or**
> **3 flour tortillas (15-inch-diameter),**
> **homemade (page 77) or purchased**
>
> 4 **cups (1 lb.) shredded *asadero* (Mexican-style string cheese), Cheddar cheese, or jack cheese**
>
> 1 **cup (about 4 oz.) coarsely crumbled *cotija* (Mexican-style dry white cheese) or 1 cup (about 5 oz.) grated Parmesan cheese**
>
> 1 **can (7 oz.) whole green chiles, seeded and cut into long, thin strips**
> **Fried Chorizo (directions follow), optional**
> **Fresh cilantro (coriander) sprigs (optional)**
> **Pickled cherry peppers (optional)**

In a wide frying pan, melt enough lard to make fat ¼ to ½ inch deep (or pour in oil to this depth). Set over high heat and bring to 375°F on a deep-frying thermometer.

Slide 1 tortilla at a time into fat (largest ones will curve up pan sides), coating top. While tortilla is still pliable, form a rim on it, using 2 sets of tongs to guide the edges up 1 to 3 inches against pan sides.

When tortilla is crisp and golden on bottom and sides are slightly rigid (2 to 3 minutes), gently tilt it with tongs to cook each rim in oil until pale gold. Using tongs, carefully transfer tortilla to paper towels and drain, cupped side down.

If you fry shells ahead, let cool, then individually wrap airtight in plastic wrap. Store at room temperature for up to 2 days.

Prepare Fried Chorizo, if desired. Sprinkle cheeses evenly inside shells. Distribute chile strips and chorizo (if used) over cheese. Place 1 shell at a time on a slightly larger baking pan.

Bake, uncovered, in a 350° oven just until cheese is melted (5 to 7 minutes). Slide tortilla onto a platter; garnish with cilantro and a cherry pepper, if desired. While 1 tortilla is being eaten, bake another. Makes 12 to 16 servings.

FRIED CHORIZO. Remove casings from ½ pound **chorizo sausages.** Crumble meat into a wide frying pan. Cook over medium-high heat, stirring, until meat is browned. Discard fat. Use meat hot or cold.

Per serving (with chorizo): 273 calories, 14 g protein, 8 g carbohydrates, 20 g total fat, 45 mg cholesterol, 665 mg sodium

Cheese-Stuffed Blossom Appetizers

Preparation time: About 30 minutes
Cooking time: 8 to 10 minutes

The bright yellow blooms of any squash—winter or summer, acorn to zucchini—can be stuffed to make an attractive, delicious appetizer.

> 15 **to 20 squash blossoms, *each* about 3 inches from base to tip**
>
> 1 **small package (3 oz.) cream cheese, at room temperature**
>
> 1 **tablespoon milk**
>
> ⅓ **cup grated Parmesan cheese**
> **Dash of pepper**
>
> 1½ **tablespoons canned diced green chiles**
> **All-purpose flour**
>
> 2 **eggs**
>
> 1 **tablespoon water**
> **Salad oil**

Rinse blossoms with a gentle spray of cool water; shake off excess. Trim off stems completely. Remove stamens, if necessary, to enlarge cavity before stuffing. Set aside.

In a bowl, blend cream cheese with milk, Parmesan cheese, pepper, and chiles. Spoon about 1 teaspoon filling into each blossom; twist tips to close. Roll blossoms in flour to coat lightly; set aside.

Beat eggs with water. Heat ¼ inch oil in a wide frying pan over medium-high heat. With a fork, dip 1 blossom at a time into egg mixture and put in pan. Fry, turning as needed, until golden brown. Drain on paper towels; keep warm until all are fried. Makes 15 to 20 appetizers.

Per appetizer: 45 calories, 2 g protein, 1 g carbohydrates, 4 g total fat, 33 mg cholesterol, 48 mg sodium

Hot from the oven, an Arizona Cheese Crisp (recipe on facing page) is ready to break into pieces and enjoy. The platter-size flour tortilla holds a pool of melted mild *asadero* cheese topped with crumbled *cotija* and green chile strips.

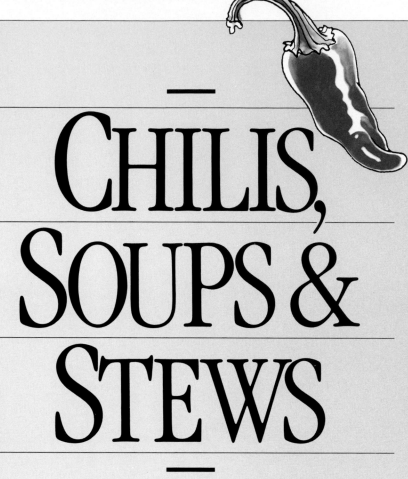

CHILIS, SOUPS & STEWS

A hearty one-pot meal with a Mexican flavor, chili is said to be an authentic American cowboy invention. Originally, it was prepared with plentiful supplies of coarsely ground chiles and beef. But today's Southwestern chili cooks can't seem to agree on how to make the best "bowl of red": Should it be made with chunks of beef or with ground meat? Should it contain beans and tomatoes? How hot should it be?

In this chapter, we offer several renditions of chili. Two traditional recipes—Santa Fe Chili with Meat and Rio Grande Chili—are made with chunks of beef and dried red chiles, with beans served on the side. Newer versions include New Mexican Red Bean Chili with ground meat, spicy J.R.'s Chili with three types of chiles and masa flour, and an unusual white bean chili flavored with pork and green chiles.

Also included in this chapter are whole-meal soups and stews. The soup selections have spicy, south-of-the-border flavors; many of the stews are mellow-flavored, rib-sticking mixtures with an Indian heritage.

J. R.'s Chili

Preparation time: About 45 minutes
Cooking time: 1¾ to 2¼ hours

Some people like their chili with beans; some insist it should be made without them. To appease both camps, we make beans optional in this version.

- 6 **dried ancho chiles**
- 1½ **cups water**
- 2 **tablespoons salad oil**
- 2 **pounds lean boneless beef, cut into 1-inch cubes**
- 3 **large red onions, chopped**
- 2 **large cloves garlic, minced or pressed**
- 1½ **teaspoons *each* paprika, salt, dry oregano leaves, and ground cumin**
- ¼ **to ½ teaspoon ground red pepper (cayenne)**
- 1 **to 3 fresh or pickled hot yellow wax chiles, sliced**
- 1 **to 3 fresh or canned jalapeño chiles, sliced**
- ½ **cup dry red wine or regular-strength beef broth**
- ¼ **cup dehydrated masa flour (corn tortilla flour) blended with ½ cup water**
- 2 **cans (about 1 lb. *each*) pinto or kidney beans, drained (optional)**

Rinse ancho chiles and discard stems; break chiles into pieces. Place chiles in a 1- to 2-quart pan with water. Bring to a boil over high heat; reduce heat, cover, and simmer until chiles are soft (about 30 minutes). Whirl chiles and their liquid in a blender or food processor until smooth; set aside.

Heat oil in a 5- to 6-quart pan over medium-high heat. Add half the meat at a time and cook, stirring as needed, until well browned. Lift out meat and set aside. Reduce heat to medium; add onions and garlic to pan and cook, stirring, until onions are soft (about 10 minutes). Return meat to pan with paprika, salt, oregano, cumin, red pepper, yellow wax and jalapeño chiles, wine, and ancho chile purée.

Bring to a boil over high heat; reduce heat, cover, and simmer until meat is tender when pierced (1½ to 2 hours).

Stir masa mixture into chili. Cook, uncovered, stirring occasionally, until mixture thickens (about 15 minutes). Stir in beans, if used, and heat through. Makes about 6 servings.

Per serving (without beans): 395 calories, 33 g protein, 21 g carbohydrates, 21 g total fat, 98 mg cholesterol, 676 mg sodium

Green Chili with White Beans

Preparation time: About 45 minutes (if starting with canned or cooked beans)
Cooking time: About 2¼ hours

White beans combine with green chiles and pork for a light, flavorful variation on the standard dish of red beans with red chiles and beef. (For a big party, you might serve a pot of each type.)

Canned beans are perfectly acceptable in this dish, but if you'd rather prepare your own, cook 2 pounds of small white beans in 4 quarts water as directed for pinto beans in Rio Grande Chile (page 24).

- 2 **large green bell peppers, seeded**
- 3 **tablespoons salad oil**
- 2 **cups sliced green onions (including tops)**
- 8 **cloves garlic, minced or pressed**
- 4 **teaspoons ground cumin**
- 6 **cans (13 oz. *each*) tomatillos**
- 4 **cans (7 oz. *each*) diced green chiles**
- 6 **cans (15 oz. *each*) Italian white beans (cannellini), drained; or 9 cups cooked small white beans, drained**
- 3 **pounds boneless pork shoulder or butt, trimmed of fat and cut into ½-inch cubes**
- 4 **teaspoons dry oregano leaves**
- ½ **teaspoon ground red pepper (cayenne)**
- ½ **cup lightly packed fresh cilantro (coriander) leaves**

Thinly slice bell peppers crosswise. Heat oil in a 10- to 12-quart pan over medium-high heat; add bell peppers, onions, garlic, and cumin. Cook, stirring, until onions are soft (about 5 minutes). Mix in tomatillos (break up with a spoon) and their liquid, chiles, beans, pork, oregano, and red pepper.

Bring to a boil; then reduce heat and simmer until pork is tender when pierced (1½ to 2 hours). For a thin chili, cook covered; for thicker chili, cook uncovered to desired consistency. Stir occasionally. (At this point, you may let cool, then cover and refrigerate for up to 3 days. Reheat before continuing.)

Reserve a few cilantro leaves; chop remaining leaves. Stir chopped cilantro into chili; garnish with reserved leaves. Makes 10 to 12 servings.

Per serving: 404 calories, 32 g protein, 41 g carbohydrates, 12 g total fat, 60 mg cholesterol, 1,547 mg sodium

Meaty bowl of Rio Grande Chili (recipe on page 24) is embellished with an array of colorful and tasty condiments—shredded Cheddar cheese, diced tomatoes, sour cream, and sliced green onions. Squares of warm cornbread make an ideal accompaniment.

22

SANTA FE CHILI WITH MEAT

Preparation time: 40 to 50 minutes
Cooking time: 3½ to 4½ hours

Black Beans (page 69), Chorizo Bread (page 85), and a crisp green salad are tasty accompaniments for this hearty, tomato-based chili. Much of the work can be done ahead, so it's a good choice for a party entrée.

 4 ounces dried red New Mexico or California chiles
 3 cups water
 ½ cup olive oil or salad oil
 2 large onions, chopped
 3 cloves garlic, minced or pressed
 5 pounds boneless beef chuck, cut into 1½-inch cubes
 ½ cup all-purpose flour
 ¼ cup chopped fresh cilantro (coriander)
 2 teaspoons *each* ground cumin, ground cloves, dry oregano leaves, dry rosemary, and dry tarragon
 2 large cans (28 oz. *each*) tomatoes
 1 can (14½ oz.) regular-strength beef broth

Rinse chiles; discard stems and seeds. Break chiles into pieces. Combine chiles and water in a 2½- to 3-quart pan. Bring to a boil over high heat; then reduce heat, cover, and simmer until chiles are soft (about 30 minutes).

In a blender, whirl chiles and their cooking liquid until puréed. With a spoon, rub purée through a fine wire strainer; discard residue. Set purée aside.

Heat oil in a 6- to 8-quart pan over medium heat; add onions and garlic and cook, stirring often, until onions are soft (about 10 minutes). Sprinkle meat with flour. Add meat and chile purée to pan and cook, stirring, for 5 minutes.

Add cilantro, cumin, cloves, oregano, rosemary, tarragon, tomatoes (break up with a spoon) and their liquid, and broth. Bring to a boil over high heat; reduce heat and simmer, uncovered, until meat is very tender when pierced (3 to 4 hours), stirring often. If made ahead, let cool; then cover and refrigerate for up to 2 days. Reheat to serve. Makes about 12 servings.

Per serving: 724 calories, 35 g protein, 18 g carbohydrates, 58 g total fat, 138 mg cholesterol, 484 mg sodium

NEW MEXICAN RED BEAN CHILI

Preparation time: 20 to 25 minutes
Cooking time: About 1 hour

Ground beef and canned kidney beans produce this speedy version of chili con carne. It gets color and medium fire from sweet red peppers and ground New Mexico chile.

 2 pounds lean ground beef
 1 large onion, chopped
 2 jars (7 oz. *each*) roasted red peppers or canned pimentos
 3½ cups regular-strength beef broth
 1 large can (28 oz.) tomatoes
 1 teaspoon ground allspice
 2 teaspoons *each* ground cumin and ground coriander
 4 teaspoons dry oregano leaves
 ½ cup ground New Mexico chile
 3 cans (about 1 lb. *each*) kidney beans, drained

Crumble beef into a 5- to 6-quart pan over high heat. Cook, stirring, until beef is well browned. Lift out meat and set aside. Discard all but 2 tablespoons of the drippings. To drippings, add onion and cook, stirring often, until onion is soft (about 10 minutes).

Meanwhile, purée peppers and their liquid in a blender or food processor until smooth. Return beef to pan with pepper purée, broth, tomatoes (break up with a spoon) and their liquid, allspice, cumin, coriander, oregano, ground chile, and beans. Bring to a boil; then reduce heat, cover, and simmer for 45 minutes. Uncover and continue to simmer until thickened to your liking (15 minutes or more); stir often. If made ahead, let cool; then cover and refrigerate for up to 2 days. Reheat to serve. Makes 6 servings.

Per serving: 646 calories, 44 g protein, 56 g carbohydrates, 29 g total fat, 95 mg cholesterol, 1,712 mg sodium

TURKEY & RED BEAN CHILI

Follow directions for **New Mexican Red Bean Chili,** but substitute **ground turkey** for the ground beef and **chicken broth** for the beef broth. Heat 2 tablespoons **salad oil** in pan before adding meat. Omit roasted red peppers and ground New Mexico chile; instead, use 2 or 3 cans (7 oz. *each*) **diced green chiles.** Makes 6 servings.

RIO GRANDE CHILI

Pictured on page 22

Preparation time: About 1½ hours; soak beans overnight
Cooking time: About 2 hours

Laden with chiles, garlic, onions, and herbs, this exceptional chili benefits from standing in the refrigerator for a day or two to blend flavors.

    Cooked Pinto Beans (directions follow)
 4 ounces dried red New Mexico or
    California chiles
 2 cans (12 oz. *each*) beer
 8 pounds bone-in beef chuck
    About 2 tablespoons salad oil
 4 large onions, chopped
 1 head garlic (about 15 cloves), minced or
    pressed
 1½ tablespoons *each* chili powder and
    paprika
 4 teaspoons ground cumin
 1 tablespoon dry oregano leaves
 1½ teaspoons sugar
 1 teaspoon ground coriander
 ½ teaspoon ground red pepper (cayenne)
 ¼ teaspoon ground allspice
 1 can (14½ oz.) regular-strength chicken
    broth
 1 can (8 oz.) tomato sauce
 2 tablespoons bourbon whiskey (optional)
    Salt
    Condiments (suggestions follow)

Soak pinto beans overnight, then cook as directed. Meanwhile, rinse chiles; discard stems and seeds. Break chiles into pieces. Combine chiles and beer in a 4- to 5-quart pan. Bring to a boil over high heat; then reduce heat, cover, and simmer until chiles are soft (about 30 minutes). Whirl chiles and their cooking liquid in a food processor or blender until puréed. With a spoon, rub purée through a fine wire strainer; discard residue. Set purée aside.

Cut beef from bones. Trim and discard excess fat; cut meat into 1-inch cubes.

Heat oil in an 8- to 10-quart pan over medium-high heat. Add meat, about ¼ at a time, and cook until well browned on all sides. Lift out meat and set aside.

Add onions and garlic to pan. Cook over medium heat, stirring often, until onions are soft (about 10 minutes). Add chili powder, paprika, cumin, oregano, sugar, coriander, red pepper, and allspice. Cook, stir-

ring, for 2 minutes. Add beef and any juices that have accumulated, chile purée, broth, tomato sauce, and whiskey, if used. Stir well, then bring to a boil over high heat; reduce heat, cover, and simmer, stirring occasionally, until beef is very tender to bite (about 2 hours). Season to taste with salt. If made ahead, let cool; then cover and refrigerate for up to 2 days. Reheat to serve. Ladle chili into individual bowls; top with beans and condiments. Makes 10 to 12 servings.

COOKED PINTO BEANS. Sort 1 pound **dried pinto beans;** remove any debris. Rinse beans and place in a large bowl; cover with **water** and let stand until next day.

Drain beans, discarding liquid. Combine beans, 8 cups **water,** and 1 **dry bay leaf** in a 5-quart pan. Bring to a boil over high heat; reduce heat, cover, and simmer until beans are very tender to bite (1 to 1½ hours). Season to taste with **salt.** Drain beans before serving.

CONDIMENTS. Arrange in separate bowls: 2 to 3 cups (8 to 12 oz.) shredded **Cheddar cheese,** 2 to 3 cups **sour cream,** 2 cups diced **tomatoes,** and 1 cup sliced **green onions** (including tops).

Per serving: 543 calories, 47 g protein, 40 g carbohydrates, 23 g total fat, 118 mg cholesterol, 429 mg sodium

CHICKEN & CHIPOTLE CHILE SOUP

Preparation time: About 30 minutes
Cooking time: About 1½ hours

This soup takes its spirited flavor from chipotle chiles and fresh cilantro. Guests may choose from a vivid assortment of toppings.

      3½- to 4-pound frying chicken
  3   quarts water
  8   cloves garlic, quartered
 10   whole black peppercorns
  ½   can (7-oz. size) chipotle chiles in
      adobo sauce, chopped
      Salt
      Toppings (suggestions follow)

Remove chicken neck and giblets; rinse. Reserve neck and liver for other uses; place remaining giblets in a 6- to 8-quart pan. Rinse chicken and discard lumps of fat; add chicken to pan. Add water, garlic, peppercorns, and chiles. Bring to a boil over high heat. Reduce heat, cover, and simmer until meat pulls easily from bones (about 1 hour).

Remove from heat and let chicken cool in broth. Shred meat and return to broth; discard skin and bones. (At this point, you may cover and refrigerate for up to 2 days.)

Skim and discard fat from soup. Bring soup to a simmer; then season to taste with salt. Offer toppings to add to individual servings. Makes 8 to 10 servings.

TOPPINGS. Arrange in separate bowls: ½ can (7-oz. size; leftover from soup) **chipotle chiles in adobo sauce** (chopped); 1 can (about 1 lb.) **garbanzo beans,** drained; 1 large firm-ripe **avocado,** pitted, peeled, thinly sliced, and sprinkled with **lime juice** to prevent darkening; 1 cup **fresh cilantro (coriander) leaves;** and 4 or 5 **limes,** cut into quarters.

Per serving: 181 calories, 20 g protein, 7 g carbohydrates, 7 g total fat, 63 mg cholesterol, 206 mg sodium

CREAM OF CHICKEN SOUP

———

Preparation time: 25 to 35 minutes
Cooking time: About 1¼ hours

Good for what ails you—that's chicken soup's claim to fame. This intriguing blend of meaty broth and cream, spiked with red pepper, is no exception.

> 3½- to 4-pound frying chicken
> 7 cups water
> 3 small onions, cut into quarters
> 3 medium-size tomatoes, peeled and cut into wedges
> ½ teaspoon *each* crushed dried hot red chiles and ground cumin
> 2 cups whipping cream
>   Salt and pepper
> ½ cup fresh cilantro (coriander) sprigs

Remove chicken neck and giblets and reserve for other uses. Rinse chicken; discard lumps of fat.

In a 6- to 8-quart pan, combine chicken, water, and onions. Bring to a boil over high heat; then reduce heat, cover, and simmer until meat pulls easily from bones (about 1 hour). Lift out chicken and let cool. Shred meat and set aside; discard skin and bones.

Boil broth over high heat, uncovered, until reduced to 4 cups. Pour broth through a wire strainer and set aside. Return onions to pan along with tomatoes, chiles, and cumin; stir over medium heat until tomatoes mash easily (about 10 minutes). Add broth, cream, and chicken and bring to boiling. Season to taste with salt and pepper.

Ladle into bowls and top with cilantro. Makes about 6 servings.

Per serving: 503 calories, 34 g protein, 12 g carbohydrates, 35 g total fat, 185 mg cholesterol, 128 mg sodium

CORN & SHRIMP SOUP

———

Preparation time: About 30 minutes
Cooking time: About 15 minutes

Chili lovers will relish the heat in this hearty soup; you can temper it slightly with cheese, or add more fire with salsa.

> 2 tablespoons butter or margarine
> 1 small onion, finely chopped
> ½ teaspoon ground cumin
> 3½ cups regular-strength chicken broth
> 1 tablespoon cornstarch
> 2½ cups fresh corn kernels (or frozen corn kernels, thawed)
> 1 large red bell pepper, seeded and chopped
> ½ to ¾ cup purchased salsa
> 1 pound medium-size shrimp, shelled and deveined
> 1½ cups (6 oz.) shredded jalapeño-flavored jack cheese

Melt butter in a 5-quart pan over medium-high heat. Add onion and cumin; cook, stirring often, until onion is soft (about 10 minutes). Blend 1 to 2 tablespoons of the broth with cornstarch; pour into pan with remaining broth, corn, bell pepper, and ¼ cup of the salsa. Bring to a boil over high heat, stirring. Add shrimp and cook until shrimp turn pink (3 to 5 minutes).

Ladle soup into 4 wide bowls. Offer cheese and remaining ¼ to ½ cup salsa at the table. Makes 4 servings.

Per serving: 441 calories, 35 g protein, 25 g carbohydrates, 21 g total fat, 183 mg cholesterol, 1,643 mg sodium

Black Bean Soup

Pictured on facing page

Preparation time: About 1½ hours
Cooking time: 3 to 3½ hours

What goes into this party-size soup is up to the diner. Guests start with thick, well-seasoned bean soup, then add their choice of colorful condiments.

 ½ **cup olive oil**
 ½ **pound salt pork or bacon, diced**
 ½ **pound Westphalian or Black Forest ham, diced, or 1 pound meaty ham hocks, cut into 2-inch pieces**
 8 **large onions, chopped**
 8 **cloves garlic, minced or pressed**
 6 **large stalks celery (including leaves, if any), chopped**
 2 **pounds (about 5 cups) dried black beans**
 ½ **teaspoon ground red pepper (cayenne)**
 4 **teaspoons ground cumin**
 4 **large cans (49½ oz. *each*) regular-strength chicken broth**
 ¼ **cup wine vinegar**
 1 **cup dry sherry**
    Condiments (suggestions follow)

Heat oil in a 10- to 12-quart pan over medium-high heat. Add salt pork, ham, onions, garlic, and celery. Cook, stirring occasionally, until vegetables are very soft and lightly browned (about 40 minutes).

Sort beans to remove debris; rinse well, drain, and add to pan along with red pepper, cumin, and broth. Bring to a boil over high heat; reduce heat, cover, and simmer until beans mash easily—2½ to 3 hours. (If using ham hocks, lift out and let cool. Shred meat and return to pan; discard skin and bones.) Skim and discard fat from soup.

Whirl soup, a portion at a time, in a food processor or blender until smooth. (At this point, you may let cool, then cover and refrigerate until next day.)

Return soup to pan and heat until steaming, stirring often. Blend in vinegar and sherry.

Pass condiments at the table to add to individual servings. Makes 20 to 24 servings.

CONDIMENTS. Arrange in separate bowls: 3 pounds warm **kielbasa** (Polish sausage), cut into ½-inch-thick slices; 4 to 6 cups **hot cooked rice;** 2 cups thinly sliced **radishes;** 8 **hard-cooked eggs,** chopped; 2 cups small **sweet pickle spears;** and 2 cups diced **green bell peppers.**

Per serving: 290 calories, 14 g protein, 29 g carbohydrates, 10 g total fat, 10 mg cholesterol, 1,266 mg sodium

Home-style Menudo

Preparation time: 35 to 45 minutes
Cooking time: 6½ to 7½ hours

Reputed to soothe the overindulgent after a wild night out, menudo is also a popular family dish. Our version can be made with supermarket ingredients.

 3½ **pounds beef tripe, rinsed well and cut into 1-inch squares**
 3 **to 3½ pounds beef shanks**
 10 **cups water**
 2 **medium-size onions, chopped**
 10 **cloves garlic, minced or pressed**
 2 **teaspoons ground cumin**
    Red Chile Purée (recipe follows)
 3 **large cans (29 oz. *each*) white or yellow hominy, drained**
    Salt
    Condiments (suggestions follow)

In an 8- to 10-quart pan, combine tripe, beef shanks, water, onions, garlic, and cumin. Bring to a boil over high heat; then reduce heat, cover, and simmer until tripe is very tender to bite (6 to 7 hours). Meanwhile, prepare Red Chile Purée; set aside.

Skim and discard fat from liquid. Lift beef shanks from pan; discard bones and fat. Cut meat into chunks and return to pan along with chile purée and hominy. Season to taste with salt. Bring to a boil; then reduce heat, cover, and simmer for 30 minutes to blend flavors. If made ahead, let cool; then cover and refrigerate for up to 2 days. To serve, reheat to simmering.

Ladle into bowls; pass condiments at the table. Makes 10 to 12 servings.

RED CHILE PURÉE. Discard stems and seeds from 9 large **dried red New Mexico or California chiles.** Place chiles in a bowl with 3¼ cups **warm water.** Let stand until softened (20 to 30 minutes). Discard all but 1¼ cups liquid. In a blender or food processor, purée chiles with liquid until smooth; scrape down sides of container once or twice.

CONDIMENTS. Arrange in separate bowls: 3 **limes** or lemons, cut into wedges; ½ cup **fresh oregano leaves;** 1 cup **fresh cilantro (coriander) sprigs;** 1 medium-size **onion,** chopped; and ¼ cup **crushed dried hot red chiles** or 5 fresh serrano or jalapeño chiles, stemmed, seeded, and thinly sliced.

Per serving: 386 calories, 47 g protein, 30 g carbohydrates, 8 g total fat, 125 mg cholesterol, 729 mg sodium

Garnished with cilantro and red chiles, steaming Black Bean Soup (recipe on facing page) is ready to serve buffet style. Alongside, offer lots of flavorful condiments—sausage, chopped egg, sweet pickles, and more.

JUNIPER LAMB STEW

Preparation time: About 30 minutes
Cooking time: About 1½ hours

Accompany this vegetable-laden Indian stew with Paper Bread (page 81) to make a contemporary family meal that reflects a much older life-style.

> 3 tablespoons all-purpose flour
> 1½ tablespoons chili powder
> 1 teaspoon salt
> ½ teaspoon pepper
> 2 pounds lean boneless lamb, cut into 1½-inch cubes
> 2 tablespoons salad oil
> 1 large onion, chopped
> 1½ to 2 cups fresh corn kernels (or frozen corn kernels, thawed)
> 3 medium-size green bell peppers, seeded and cut into ¾-inch squares
> 2 large tomatoes, coarsely chopped
> 1 stalk celery, thinly sliced
> 2 tablespoons crushed dry juniper berries
> 3 cans (14½ oz. *each*) regular-strength beef broth
> Chopped green onions (including tops)

In a bag, combine flour, chili powder, salt, and pepper. Add meat and shake to coat evenly.

Heat oil in a 5- to 6-quart pan over medium-high heat; add meat, a portion at a time, and cook until well browned. Add onion and continue to cook, stirring often, until onion is soft (about 10 minutes).

Add corn, bell peppers, tomatoes, celery, juniper berries, and broth. Bring to a boil over high heat; then reduce heat, cover, and simmer until meat is very tender when pierced (about 1½ hours).

Ladle into wide bowls and pass green onions to add to each serving. Makes 6 servings.

Per serving: 377 calories, 35 g protein, 21 g carbohydrates, 19 g total fat, 105 mg cholesterol, 1,345 mg sodium

INDIAN BEAN & LAMB STEW

Preparation time: About 15 minutes
Cooking time: 1½ to 2 hours

Centuries ago, Indians in the Southwest were making simple, wholesome stews similar to this

one. Sturdy Ash Bread (page 81) is a traditional accompaniment.

> 1 pound dried pinto beans
> 2 large lamb shanks (about 2 lbs. *total*)
> 1 large onion, chopped
> 3 cloves garlic, minced or pressed
> 1 tablespoon coriander seeds, crushed
> ½ teaspoon coarsely ground pepper
> 6 cups water
> Salt
> 2 to 3 medium-size tomatoes, chopped
> 1 cup chopped green onions (including tops)

Sort beans to remove debris; rinse well and drain. In a 5-quart pan, combine beans, lamb, onion, garlic, coriander seeds, pepper, and water. Bring to a boil over high heat; then reduce heat, cover, and simmer until beans are tender to bite (1½ to 2 hours), stirring occasionally.

Lift lamb from pan; discard bones and fat, then cut meat into bite-size pieces and return to pan. Skim fat from broth; season stew to taste with salt.

Spoon stew into bowls and pass tomatoes and green onions to add to each serving. Makes 6 servings.

Per serving: 462 calories, 32 g protein, 55 g carbohydrates, 13 g total fat, 54 mg cholesterol, 61 mg sodium

RED CHILE STEW

Preparation time: 20 to 30 minutes
Cooking time: 2 to 2½ hours

Offer hot steamed rice to spoon into individual servings of this spicy beef stew. Serve our Orange & Avocado Salad with Cumin Vinaigrette (page 72) alongside.

> About ⅓ cup salad oil
> 2 beef round steaks (about 2½ lbs. *each*), cut into ½-inch cubes
> 2 tablespoons all-purpose flour
> 4 cups water
> 2 large cans (28 oz. *each*) tomatoes
> 4 cloves garlic, minced or pressed
> 4 teaspoons dry oregano leaves
> ⅓ to ½ cup ground New Mexico chile
> Salt

Heat ⅓ cup oil in a 5- to 6-quart pan over high heat. Add about ¼ of the meat and cook, stirring often, until well browned. Lift from pan and set aside. Repeat to brown remaining meat, adding more oil as needed.

Return all meat to pan; sprinkle with flour and cook, stirring, for about 1 minute. Stir in water and tomatoes (break up with a spoon) and their liquid. Add garlic and oregano. Bring to a boil over high heat; reduce heat, cover, and simmer until meat is very tender when pierced (1½ to 2 hours).

Stir in ground chile; cover and continue to cook, stirring occasionally, for 30 more minutes. Season to taste with salt. Skim and discard fat from stew. Makes about 12 servings.

Per serving: 432 calories, 43 g protein, 10 g carbohydrates, 24 g total fat, 114 mg cholesterol, 361 mg sodium

GREEN CHILE STEW

Follow directions for **Red Chile Stew,** but decrease tomatoes to 2 cans (1 lb. *each*) and omit oregano and ground chile. Instead, use 4 or 5 cans (7 oz. *each*) **diced green chiles.** Makes about 12 servings.

BUFFALO STEW

Preparation time: About 45 minutes
Cooking time: About 15 minutes

Full-flavored buffalo meat shows up in supermarkets more often than you might expect. It's typically sold as ground meat patties, usually in the freezer case.

> 2 **large onions, chopped**
> 2 **tablespoons olive oil or salad oil**
> ¾ **pound mushrooms, thinly sliced**
> 1 **pound ground buffalo or lean ground beef**
> 2 **cans (13 oz. *each*) tomatillos**
> 1 **can (15½ oz.) hominy, drained**
> 1 **can (15 oz.) baby corn, drained**
> ¼ **cup chopped fresh cilantro (coriander)**
> 1 **tablespoon dry oregano leaves**
> 5 **small dried hot red chiles**

In a 5- to 6-quart pan over medium heat, combine onions and 1 tablespoon of the oil; stir often until onions are light golden and sweet to taste (about 20 minutes). Add mushrooms and stir occasionally until liquid evaporates (about 10 more minutes). Pour mixture out of pan; set aside.

Add remaining 1 tablespoon oil to pan along with buffalo; stir frequently over high heat until meat is well browned and crumbly (about 10 minutes).

Return onion mixture to pan along with tomatillos (break up with a spoon) and their liquid; stir to free browned bits. Add hominy, corn, cilantro, oregano, and chiles; bring to a boil. Reduce heat, cover, and simmer for about 15 minutes, stirring occasionally to blend flavors. If made ahead, let cool; then cover and refrigerate until next day. Reheat to serve. Spoon out and discard hot chiles before serving, if desired. Makes 4 to 6 servings.

Per serving: 388 calories, 19 g protein, 31 g carbohydrates, 23 g total fat, 57 mg cholesterol, 362 mg sodium

BEEF & PORK PICADO

Preparation time: 25 to 30 minutes
Cooking time: About 2¾ hours

On a chilly winter evening, offer this meaty stew with Black Beans (page 69), warm, soft corn tortillas, and a crisp green salad.

> 2 **pounds *each* lean boneless beef chuck and boneless pork butt or shoulder**
> 2 **medium-size onions, cut into wedges**
> 2 **medium-size green bell peppers, seeded and cut into large chunks**
> 2 **cups regular-strength beef broth**
> 4 **medium-size tomatoes, cut into wedges**
> 4 **cloves garlic, minced or pressed**
> 1 **fresh or pickled jalapeño chile, including seeds, minced**
> ¼ **teaspoon pepper**
> **Salt**

Cut beef and pork, including any fat, into 1½-inch cubes; place in a 5- to 6-quart pan. Cover and cook over medium-high heat to draw out juices (about 10 minutes). Uncover and cook over high heat until liquid evaporates; stir occasionally. Add onions and bell peppers; cook, stirring frequently, until meat is evenly browned. Add broth, tomatoes, garlic, chile, and pepper; stir to free browned bits from pan bottom.

Reduce heat, cover, and simmer until meat is tender enough to shred easily with a fork (about 2½ hours).

Uncover and boil over medium-high heat until juices are reduced to just below top of meat and are slightly thickened, stirring more frequently as mixture thickens. Season to taste with salt. Makes about 8 servings.

Per serving: 410 calories, 45 g protein, 6 g carbohydrates, 22 g total fat, 151 mg cholesterol, 405 mg sodium

Ham, chicken, and golden hominy come together in Pozole, a popular Southwestern stew (recipe on facing page). Crunchy fried tortilla strips and condiments such as diced cream cheese, red bell peppers, and lime offer pleasing texture and flavor contrasts.

POZOLE

Pictured on facing page

Preparation time: About 45 minutes
Cooking time: About 2½ hours

In the Southwest, pozole is often made with dried or partially cooked frozen hominy, but our version uses more readily available canned hominy.

> 2 **large cans (49½ oz. *each*) regular-strength chicken broth**
> 3 **pounds meaty ham hocks, cut into 1-inch-thick slices**
> 2 **pounds chicken drumsticks and thighs**
> 1 **teaspoon dry oregano leaves**
> ½ **teaspoon cumin seeds**
> 2 **large onions, cut into chunks**
> **Condiments (suggestions follow)**
> **Crisp Tortilla Strips (recipe follows)**
> 1 **large can (29 oz.) yellow hominy, drained**
> **Purchased green chile salsa**

In a 6- to 8-quart pan, combine broth, ham, chicken, oregano, cumin seeds, and onions. Bring to a boil over high heat; then reduce heat, cover, and simmer until meat is tender when pierced (about 2 hours). Lift out meat and set aside. Pour broth through a wire strainer and return to pan. When ham hocks and chicken are cool enough to handle, discard skin, bones, and fat; tear meat into chunks and return to broth. Discard onions. (At this point, you may cover and refrigerate for up to 2 days.)

Prepare condiments and Crisp Tortilla Strips.

Skim and discard fat from broth; bring broth to a simmer. Stir in hominy; cover and cook for 30 minutes. Serve hot; offer condiments, salsa, and tortilla strips to add to each serving. Makes 8 to 10 servings.

CONDIMENTS. Arrange in separate bowls or on plates: 2 or 3 **limes,** cut into wedges; 2 small packages (3 oz. *each*) **cream cheese,** diced; 2 cups shredded **iceberg lettuce;** 1 to 1½ cups thinly sliced **green onions** (including tops); and 2 large **red bell peppers,** seeded and cut into slivers.

CRISP TORTILLA STRIPS. Stack 8 to 10 **corn tortillas** (6- to 7-inch-diameter) and cut into ¼-inch-wide strips. In a 3- to 4-quart pan, heat about 1 inch **salad oil** to 375°F on a deep-frying thermometer. Fry a handful of strips at a time, stirring often, until crisp and lightly browned (about 1 minute). Lift out; drain on paper towels. Sprinkle with **salt.**

Per serving: 245 calories, 22 g protein, 14 g carbohydrates, 8 g total fat, 61 mg cholesterol, 2,106 mg sodium

PORK STEW WITH PURSLANE

Preparation time: About 45 minutes
Cooking time: About 3 hours

Mildly tart purslane is a sprawling weed that is common in the West in late spring. Sometimes it's sold in Mexican markets as *verdolaga*. When it's unavailable, substitute spinach.

> 4½ **to 5 pounds boneless pork shoulder**
> 4 **cloves garlic**
> 2 **cups water**
> **Tomatillo Sauce (recipe follows)**
> **Salt**
> 8 **to 10 cups (about 1½ lbs.) purslane (*verdolaga*) sprigs or 3½ quarts (about 1½ lbs.) lightly packed spinach leaves**
> 3 **quarts boiling water**

Trim excess fat from pork; reserve for Tomatillo Sauce. Cut meat into 1½-inch cubes; put into a 5- to 6-quart ovenproof pan with garlic and the 2 cups water. Bring to a boil over high heat; then reduce heat, cover, and simmer for 45 minutes.

Remove from heat and ladle out 2 cups broth; reserve for sauce. Bake meat in pan, uncovered, in a 425° oven until well browned (about 1 hour). Stir often. Meanwhile, prepare Tomatillo Sauce; set aside.

Return pork to direct heat; add Tomatillo Sauce and season to taste with salt. Stir to free browned bits. Bring to a boil over high heat; then reduce heat, cover, and simmer until meat is very tender when pierced—about 1 hour. (At this point, you may let cool, then cover and refrigerate for up to 3 days. Reheat to simmering before continuing.)

Rinse purslane well; drain in a colander. Pour boiling water over greens to wilt them.

Ladle stew into bowls; top with greens. Makes 8 to 10 servings.

TOMATILLO SAUCE. In a blender or food processor, purée 3 cans (13 oz. *each*) **tomatillos,** drained, and 4 **fresh or canned jalapeño chiles** (stemmed and seeded); set aside.

In a 12- to 14-inch frying pan over medium heat, render ¼ cup fat from **reserved pork fat;** discard extra fat. Add 4 large **onions,** sliced, and 3 cloves **garlic,** minced or pressed. Stir until onions are golden. Add the 2 cups **reserved broth;** boil, uncovered, until almost all broth has evaporated. Pour in tomatillo mixture. Use hot or cold.

Per serving: 388 calories, 38 g protein, 12 g carbohydrates, 20 g total fat, 125 mg cholesterol, 419 mg sodium

TORTILLA & TAMALE TREATS

Introduced by Mexican settlers centuries ago, tortillas are the foundation for many Southwestern dishes. Served soft, they can be wrapped around a spicy meat, bean, or cheese filling and shaped into a burrito, enchilada, or quesadilla. Crisply fried, they provide the base for half-moon-shaped tacos, stuffed chimichangas, or tall tostada towers.

Since both corn and flour tortillas are readily available in the Southwest and much of the rest of the country, our recipes are based on the purchased products. If you want to make your own, turn to page 77 for recipes.

Masa, the Mexican corn dough used to shape tortillas, is the basis for another Southwestern specialty—tamales. Tamales are made by spreading a thin layer of masa on a dried corn husk and adding a meat or cheese filling, then tying the husk into a neat bundle for steam-cooking.

Favorite Southwestern tamales include small *tamalitos,* often served alongside barbecued meats, and "green" tamales made with fresh summer corn.

Salsas and sauces to accompany tortilla and tamale dishes, as well as many other recipes in this book, are also featured in this chapter.

Green Corn Tamales

Pictured on page 35

Preparation time: About 1 1/2 hours
Cooking time: About 1 hour

An abundant supply of sweet summer corn in the Southwest signals the time for a favorite treat—green corn tamales. They aren't literally green; they get that name because they cook in fresh green corn husks. The filling is made by grinding and seasoning fresh sweet corn. When steamed, these tamales taste like a delicate corn pudding.

- **5** or **6 medium-size ears corn in husks (about 5 lbs. *total*)**
- **¼ cup lard or solid vegetable shortening, melted**
- **2 teaspoons sugar**
  Salt
- **¾ cup shredded Longhorn Cheddar cheese**
- **⅓ cup (half a 4-oz. can) canned diced green chiles or canned whole green chiles cut into thin slivers**

With a sharp knife or cleaver, cutting through husk, corn, and cob of each ear of corn, remove about ¼ inch on both ends of ear.

Peel off husks without tearing them; rinse if soiled. To keep moist, put in plastic bags and seal; set aside. Pull silk from corn and discard; rinse corn.

With a knife or a corn scraper, cut kernels from cobs; you need 4 cups, lightly packed. Put corn through a food chopper fitted with a fine blade, or whirl in a food processor until finely ground. Mix with lard and sugar; season to taste with salt. Stir cheese and chiles into corn.

To shape each tamale, center 1⅓ tablespoons of the cheese-corn filling near stem (firmer) end of a large single husk. Fold 1 side of husk over to completely cover filling, then fold other side over top. Fold up flexible end to seal in filling. Gently stack tamales, folded end down, on a rack in a steamer; support them against other tamales so ends stay shut.

Steam tamales over 1 inch of boiling water in a covered pan until centers are firm to touch, not runny (about 1 hour); remove a tamale and unwrap to test. Add boiling water as required to maintain water level.

Serve at once, or keep warm in steamer for up to an hour. To freeze, let cool completely, then place a single layer on baking sheets; when frozen solid, transfer to plastic bags and store in freezer for up to 6 months. To reheat, let thaw, then steam as directed for about 15 minutes. Makes 3 dozen tamales (3 to 6 servings).

Per serving: 230 calories, 7 g protein, 22 g carbohydrates, 14 g total fat, 23 mg cholesterol, 150 mg sodium

Small Cheese Tamales

Preparation time: About 2 hours to soak husks; 1 1/2 hours to assemble
Cooking time: About 45 minutes

Big and small tamales have been a part of Southwestern cuisine since the hacienda days of Spanish and Mexican rule. Large entrée-size tamales are usually reserved for special holidays, but *tamalitos* like these are often served at barbecue meals.

- **30 to 36 nicely shaped corn husks**
  Masa Dough (recipe follows)
- **8 ounces jack cheese, cut into 24 cubes**
- **2 tablespoons ground New Mexico chile or other chili powder, 24 small fresh epazote leaves, or 1 tablespoon dried epazote**
  Salsa Fresca (page 40) or 1 jar (12 oz.) green chile salsa

Soak corn husks (see page 10) and prepare Masa Dough. Sort through husks and select 24 that are at least 5 inches wide across base and free of holes or large tears.

Working with 1 husk at a time, spread it out flat and put a scant 2 tablespoons of masa in center. Push 1 cube of cheese and ¼ teaspoon ground chile (or 1 small epazote leaf or ⅛ teaspoon dried epazote) into masa.

With fingers, pat masa up and around cheese and seasoning. Fold sides of husk over masa, then lift ends up over filling. With a thin strip of husk, tie tamale to hold shut. Repeat to make 23 more tamales. (At this point, you may cover and refrigerate until next day.)

Set tamales, tied ends up, stacked to permit air circulation, in a steamer on a rack over at least 1 inch of boiling water. Cover and set heat at medium so water will boil gently (add boiling water to pan as required). Cook until masa is firm to touch and does not stick to husk (about 45 minutes); open a tamale to test, then retie. Serve, or keep warm in steamer for up to an hour. If made ahead, let cool, then cover and refrigerate until next day; reheat by steaming as directed for about 20 minutes.

To serve, open husks and spoon salsa to taste onto tamales. Makes 2 dozen tamales (6 to 8 servings).

Masa Dough. Whip ⅔ cup **lard,** butter, margarine, or solid vegetable shortening until fluffy, then stir in 2 cups **dehydrated masa flour** (corn tortilla flour) and 1⅓ cups **regular-strength chicken or beef broth.** Stir until mixture holds together. If made ahead, cover and refrigerate for up to 3 days; bring to room temperature before using.

Per serving: 399 calories, 11 g protein, 23 g carbohydrates, 29 g total fat, 43 mg cholesterol, 567 mg sodium

BLUE CORN TAMALE PIE

Preparation time: About 2½ hours to prepare meat sauce and crust
Baking time: About 20 minutes

The crust for this open-faced tamale pie is made with blue cornmeal; the spicy filling is also used in our Flat Blue Enchiladas (page 42).

Red Chile Pork Sauce (recipe follows)
1½ **cups blue cornmeal for tortillas (harina para tortillas)**
3½ **cups regular-strength chicken broth**
3 **cups (12 oz.) shredded Cheddar cheese**
½ **to ¾ cup sour cream**

Prepare Red Chile Pork Sauce. Pour sauce into a 10- to 12-inch frying pan. Bring to a boil over high heat; then reduce heat and simmer, uncovered, stirring often, until sauce is reduced to 2½ cups. Set aside.

In a 3- to 4-quart pan, combine cornmeal and broth. Stirring, bring to a boil over high heat and cook until mixture is very thick (10 to 12 minutes). At once, spread mixture evenly over bottom and sides of a shallow 3-quart casserole.

Spoon sauce into cornmeal crust. Bake, uncovered, in a 350° oven until very hot in center (about 10 minutes). Sprinkle with cheese and continue baking until cheese is melted (10 more minutes). Pass sour cream to spoon on top. Makes 6 servings.

RED CHILE PORK SAUCE. Roast 6 to 8 **dried red New Mexico or California chiles** in a 300° oven until they smell slightly toasted (about 4 minutes). Discard stems and seeds. Place chiles in a 3- to 4-quart pan with 5 cups **water.** Bring to a boil; then reduce heat and simmer, uncovered, until soft (20 to 25 minutes). Drain, reserving liquid. Whirl chiles in a blender with ½ cup cooking liquid until smoothly puréed.

Cut 1 pound **lean boneless pork butt** or shoulder into 1½-inch cubes. Place pork in a 2- to 3-quart pan over medium heat; cover and cook to draw out juices (about 10 minutes). Uncover and cook over high heat, stirring often, until liquid evaporates and meat is well browned. Add 2 cups **water,** stirring to scrape up browned bits in pan. Bring to a boil; then reduce heat, cover, and simmer until meat is very tender when pierced (1 to 1¼ hours). Uncover; boil over high heat until liquid evaporates, stirring often. Remove from heat; shred meat with 2 forks.

Melt 2 tablespoons **butter** or margarine in a 12- to 14-inch frying pan over medium heat. Add 1 large **onion,** chopped, and 1 clove **garlic,** minced or pressed. Stir often until onion is soft (about 10 minutes). Add pork, chile purée, 4 cups reserved chile cooking liquid (add water if necessary), ½ teaspoon

dry oregano leaves, and ¼ teaspoon **ground cumin.** Bring to a boil over high heat; then reduce heat and simmer, uncovered, stirring often, until reduced to 3 cups. Season to taste with **salt.** If made ahead, let cool, then cover and refrigerate for up to 3 days.

Per serving: 513 calories, 22 g protein, 37 g carbohydrates, 32 g total fat, 83 mg cholesterol, 862 mg sodium

SIX-FOOT BURRITO

Preparation time: About 3 hours to prepare salsa and chili; 10 to 20 minutes to assemble burrito

For a casual dinner party, try this eye-catching burrito made with homemade or purchased chili and plenty of colorful toppings.

Blender Salsa (page 41)
8 **cups Rio Grande Chili (page 24), made without beans; or 3 cans (about 30 oz. each) chili without beans**
12 **to 18 flour tortillas (about 8-inch-diameter)**
2 **cups chopped onions**
5 **cups (1¼ lbs.) shredded jack or Cheddar cheese**
2 **large heads butter lettuce, washed and separated into leaves**
2 **cups cherry tomatoes, cut in half**
1 **cup thinly sliced green onions (including tops)**
2 **cups sour cream**
1½ **to 2 cups Guacamole (page 16)**

Prepare Blender Salsa (cover and refrigerate) and Rio Grande Chili (if used). Bring chili to a boil over medium heat, stirring.

To assemble burrito, overlap tortillas down the length of a clean 1 by 12 board, 6 to 7 feet long. Ladle chili down center in a 2-inch-wide band. Sprinkle on chopped onions and 3 cups of the cheese.

Bring 1 side of tortillas up over filling, then roll to enclose, tucking seam underneath. (It's advisable to have several helpers working down length of burrito.)

Tuck lettuce leaves under burrito on both sides; garnish with tomato halves and remaining 2 cups cheese.

To serve, cut burrito into 3- to 4-inch sections; transfer to individual plates with a wide spatula. Let guests top servings with Blender Salsa, green onions, sour cream, and Guacamole to taste. Eat with knife and fork. Makes 20 to 24 servings.

Per serving: 648 calories, 54 g protein, 37 g carbohydrates, 32 g total fat, 149 mg cholesterol, 503 mg sodium

Miniature in size and mild in flavor, these steamed Green Corn Tamales
(recipe on page 33) make an ideal companion for slices of hearty
barbecued beef served with Salsa Fresca (recipe on page 40).

TACOS PESCADO

Preparation time: About 20 minutes
Cooking time: About 15 minutes for tortillas; 10 minutes for fish

To prepare the light *pescado* (fish) filling for these tacos, simply poach red snapper fillets in broth seasoned with lemon and chile.

Green Cilantro Salsa (page 40)
2 **tablespoons lemon juice**
1 **small dried hot red chile**
2 **tablespoons chopped fresh cilantro (coriander)**
1 **can (14½ oz.) regular-strength chicken broth**
1 **pound red snapper or other firm, white-fleshed fish fillets, 1 inch thick**
Salad oil
8 **corn tortillas (6- to 7-inch-diameter) or 8 purchased fried taco shells**
About 4 cups shredded lettuce
About ¾ cup sour cream

Prepare Green Cilantro Salsa; cover and refrigerate.

In a 10- to 12-inch frying pan, combine lemon juice, chile, cilantro, and broth. Bring to a boil over high heat. Arrange fillets in broth, overlapping if necessary. Return broth to boiling; then reduce heat, cover, and simmer until fish flakes when prodded with a fork in thickest part (about 10 minutes). Drain fish well; break into 1-inch chunks and keep warm.

In an 8- to 10-inch frying pan, heat ½ inch oil over medium-high heat. When oil is hot, add 1 tortilla at a time; cook, turning once, until soft (about 10 seconds *total*). Fold tortilla in half; holding slightly open with tongs, continue to fry, turning once, until crisp (1 more minute). Drain on paper towels.

To assemble each taco, place a fried tortilla on a plate; spoon chunks of fish into tortilla, then add salsa, lettuce, and sour cream. Makes 4 servings.

Per serving: 482 calories, 30 g protein, 31 g carbohydrates, 26 g total fat, 81 mg cholesterol, 667 mg sodium

GIANT FLOUR TORTILLA TACOS

Preparation time: 30 to 40 minutes
Cooking time: About 15 minutes for tortillas; 15 to 20 minutes for filling

Plate-size flour tortillas are fried and gently folded in half to make dramatic containers for this knife-and-fork entrée.

Salad oil
6 **to 8 large flour tortillas (about 12-inch-diameter)**
Beef Filling (recipe follows)
6 **to 8 cups shredded lettuce**
Garnishes (suggestions follow)

In a 12- to 14-inch frying pan, heat ½ inch oil over medium-high heat. When oil is hot, add 1 tortilla at a time; cook, turning quickly with 2 spatulas, until bubbly and just golden but still flexible (about 30 seconds). Bend tortilla in half at about a 45° angle as you lift it from oil. Drain on paper towels, leaning tortilla against something sturdy (such as a 28-oz. can) so it holds its shape as it cools. While tortillas are cooling, prepare Beef Filling.

To assemble each taco, place a fried tortilla on a plate; cover bottom with 1 cup lettuce. Spoon on about 1 cup Beef Filling, then add garnishes as desired. Serve with knife and fork to eat like a salad; break off top section of tortilla and eat it like bread. Makes 6 to 8 servings.

BEEF FILLING. Crumble 3 pounds **lean ground beef** into a wide frying pan. Cook over medium-high heat, stirring often, until meat is browned. Pour off fat. Add 2 large **onions,** chopped; cook, stirring often, until soft (about 10 minutes). Stir in 4 teaspoons **chili powder,** 1½ teaspoons *each* **dry oregano leaves** and **paprika,** ¾ teaspoon *each* **ground cumin** and **pepper,** 1 tablespoon **Worcestershire,** and 1 can (15 oz.) **tomato sauce.** Simmer, uncovered, until hot; stir often. Season to taste with **garlic salt.**

GARNISHES. Arrange in separate containers: 2 or 3 small **tomatoes,** sliced; 1 or 2 **avocados,** pitted, peeled, sliced, and sprinkled with **lemon or lime juice** to prevent darkening; jumbo **pitted ripe olives;** large **radishes; sour cream;** and **fresh cilantro (coriander) sprigs.**

Per serving: 589 calories, 36 g protein, 36 g carbohydrates, 34 g total fat, 103 mg cholesterol, 456 mg sodium

QUESADILLA

Preparation time: 5 to 10 minutes
Cooking time: About 5 minutes

Serve one or two of these simple Mexican cheese treats as a nutritious snack, or pair with Garden Gazpacho (page 13) for a light supper.

1 **teaspoon butter or margarine**
1 **flour tortilla (about 8-inch-diameter)**
2 **to 3 ounces sliced *asadero* (Mexican-style string cheese) or jack cheese**

1 tablespoon grated *cotija* (Mexican-style dry white cheese) or Parmesan cheese

1 tablespoon minced green onion (including top)

1 teaspoon minced fresh or canned hot chile

Melt butter in a 10- to 12-inch frying pan over medium-high heat, swirling pan to distribute butter. Add tortilla and top with cheeses, onion, and chile. When tortilla is warm but still flexible, fold in half; continue cooking, turning often, until cheese is melted and tortilla is browned (about 3 minutes). Serve hot. Makes 1 quesadilla.

Per quesadilla: 472 calories, 26 g protein, 19 g carbohydrates, 33 g total fat, 89 mg cholesterol, 589 mg sodium

OVEN-FRIED CHIMICHANGAS

———

Preparation time: About 25 minutes
Cooking time: About 1¾ hours for filling; 15 minutes to bake chimichangas

Chimichangas—meat-filled flour tortillas—are usually deep-fried to make them flaky and crisp. But this oven-fried version is equally delicious and much less fuss to prepare. Serve chimichangas with a fresh fruit salad.

Salsa Fresca (page 40)

1 pound lean boneless pork butt or shoulder, trimmed of excess fat and cut into 1½-inch cubes

2 cups water

2 tablespoons white vinegar

3 tablespoons canned diced green chiles

1 clove garlic, minced or pressed

¼ teaspoon *each* ground oregano and ground cumin

Salt

4 flour tortillas (about 8-inch-diameter)

3 tablespoons butter or margarine, melted

1½ cups (6 oz.) shredded jack cheese

1 cup sour cream

Prepare Salsa Fresca; cover and refrigerate.

Place meat in a 2- to 3-quart pan. Cover and cook over medium heat to draw out juices (about 10 minutes). Uncover and cook over high heat, stirring often, until liquid has evaporated and meat is well browned.

Add water to pan, stirring to scrape up browned bits. Bring to a boil over high heat; then reduce heat, cover, and simmer until meat is very tender when pierced (1 to 1¼ hours). Uncover; boil over high heat until all liquid has evaporated. Reduce heat to low.

Add vinegar, chiles, garlic, oregano, and cumin. Stir to scrape up browned bits; remove from heat.

Shred meat with 2 forks. Season to taste with salt. (At this point, you may cover and refrigerate for up to 3 days; reheat before using.)

To assemble each chimichanga, brush both sides of a tortilla with melted butter. Spoon filling down center of tortilla. To enclose, lap ends over filling; then fold sides to center to make a packet. Set chimichangas, seam side down, in a 9- by 13-inch baking pan. Bake in a 500° oven until golden (8 to 10 minutes).

Pass cheese, salsa, and sour cream to spoon on individual servings. Makes 4 servings.

Per serving: 457 calories, 15 g protein, 21 g carbohydrates, 35 g total fat, 86 mg cholesterol, 386 mg sodium

CRAB TOSTADAS

———

Preparation time: 20 to 30 minutes
Cooking time: About 10 minutes

Cooks from Southern California inspired this delicate Dungeness crab and avocado tostada. Serve it as a festive entrée at a patio brunch or supper.

Tomatillo Salsa (page 40) or purchased taco sauce

Salad oil

4 flour tortillas (about 8-inch-diameter)

1 large ripe avocado

2 tablespoons lime juice

Salt

1 can (about 1 lb.) refried beans, heated

1 cup (4 oz.) shredded Cheddar cheese

4 cups shredded lettuce

1 pound crabmeat

2 medium-size tomatoes, sliced

½ cup pitted ripe olives

Prepare Tomatillo Salsa; cover and refrigerate.

In a 10- to 12-inch frying pan, heat ½ inch oil over medium-high heat. When oil is hot, add 1 tortilla at a time; cook, turning once, until tortilla is crisp and golden brown (about 1 minute *total*). Drain on paper towels.

Pit, peel, and slice avocado. Add lime juice and mash mixture with a fork. Season to taste with salt.

Place tortillas on plates; spread evenly with beans, then sprinkle with cheese, lettuce, and crabmeat. Garnish with avocado, tomatoes, and olives. Pass salsa to spoon on tostadas. Makes 4 servings.

Per serving: 657 calories, 40 g protein, 46 g carbohydrates, 37 g total fat, 143 mg cholesterol, 963 mg sodium

Fried in hot oil until bubbly and flexible, flour tortillas are easily shaped into open "envelopes" for this Tostada Beef Salad (recipe on facing page). Top the rare beef with olives, onion, and tomatoes; garnish with radishes, if you like.

TOSTADA BEEF SALAD

Pictured on facing page

Preparation time: 35 to 45 minutes
Cooking time: About 10 minutes

Pile thinly sliced rare roast beef on a crisp-fried flour tortilla, then embellish with lettuce, vegetables, and a piquant cilantro dressing.

> **Cilantro Vinaigrette (recipe follows)**
> **Salad oil**
> 4 **flour tortillas (about 8-inch-diameter)**
> **About 1 pound thinly sliced cold rare roast beef**
> 2 **to 4 cups shredded lettuce**
> 2 **medium-size tomatoes, thinly sliced**
> ½ **small red onion, thinly sliced and separated into rings**
> **Fresh cilantro (coriander) sprigs**
> **Sliced ripe olives**

Prepare Cilantro Vinaigrette; set aside.

In a 10- to 12-inch frying pan, heat ½ inch oil over medium-high heat. When oil is hot, add 1 tortilla at a time; cook, turning quickly with 2 spatulas, until bubbly and just golden but still flexible (about 30 seconds). Bend tortilla in half at about a 45° angle as you lift it from oil. Drain on paper towels, leaning tortilla against something sturdy (such as a 28-oz. can) so it holds its shape as it cools.

To assemble each tostada, place a fried tortilla on a plate. Top flat surface with ¼ of the beef, lettuce, tomatoes, and onion. Garnish with cilantro sprigs and olives. Pass vinaigrette to drizzle over individual servings. Makes 4 servings.

Per serving: 467 calories, 34 g protein, 22 g carbohydrates, 27 g total fat, 94 mg cholesterol, 80 mg sodium

CILANTRO VINAIGRETTE. Combine ¾ cup **salad oil;** ½ cup **red wine vinegar;** 1 teaspoon **dry mustard;** 1 clove **garlic,** minced or pressed; ¼ cup chopped **fresh cilantro** (coriander); and ⅛ teaspoon **ground red pepper** (cayenne). Stir or shake well.

Per tablespoon: 74 calories, .02 g protein, .26 g carbohydrates, 8 g total fat, 0 mg cholesterol, 1 mg sodium

SHREDDED BEEF ENCHILADAS

Preparation time: About 2½ hours
Cooking time: 10 minutes for tortillas; 20 to 30 minutes to bake enchiladas

These succulent beef enchiladas belie their original Mexican name, *ropas viejas,* ("old rags"). The secret of their moistness is a sour cream and chile sauce that gets wrapped up with the shredded beef.

> 2 **pounds boneless beef chuck**
> ¼ **cup water**
> 3 **tablespoons red wine vinegar**
> 1½ **cups regular-strength beef broth**
> 2 **tablespoons chili powder**
> 1½ **teaspoons ground cumin**
> **Salad oil**
> 1 **small onion, chopped**
> 2 **cans (7 oz. *each*) diced green chiles**
> 1 **tablespoon all-purpose flour**
> 2 **cups sour cream**
> 3 **cups (12 oz.) shredded jack cheese**
> **Salt**
> 12 **corn tortillas (6- to 7-inch-diameter)**

Trim and discard most of fat from beef, then place beef in a 5- to 6-quart pan with water. Cover and cook over medium heat for 30 minutes. Uncover and cook, turning as needed, until liquid evaporates and meat is well browned.

In a bowl, combine vinegar, broth, chili powder, and 1 teaspoon of the cumin; pour over meat. Continue cooking over medium heat until meat is very tender and pulls apart easily (about 2 hours). Let meat cool; then shred and mix with pan juices.

Meanwhile, in an 8- to 10-inch frying pan, combine 2 tablespoons oil, onion, chiles, and remaining ½ teaspoon cumin. Cook over medium heat, stirring occasionally, until onion is soft (about 10 minutes). Stir in flour; then blend in 1 cup of the sour cream and stir until simmering. Remove from heat and blend in 1 cup of the cheese. Season to taste with salt. Set aside.

In a wide frying pan, heat ½ inch oil over medium-high heat. When oil is hot, add 1 tortilla at a time and cook, turning once, just until limp (about 10 seconds *total*). Drain on paper towels.

While tortillas are warm, spoon about ⅓ cup sour cream sauce and ¼ cup shredded beef down center of each; roll to enclose. Set enchiladas, seam side down, in a 10- by 15-inch baking pan. (At this point, you may cover and refrigerate until next day.)

Bake, uncovered, in a 375° oven until hot in center (about 15 minutes; 25 minutes if refrigerated). Sprinkle remaining 2 cups cheese evenly on top. Return to oven until cheese is melted (about 5 more minutes).

Use a wide spatula to transfer enchiladas to dinner plates. Pass remaining 1 cup sour cream to spoon on individual servings. Makes about 6 servings.

Per serving: 799 calories, 45 g protein, 35 g carbohydrates, 54 g total fat, 148 mg cholesterol, 1,112 mg sodium

SALSAS & SAUCES

Fresh vegetable and fruit salsas and spicy simmered sauces are vital seasonings for many Southwestern dishes, adding exciting flavor to everything from tamales to vegetables to meats.

The salsas we present here are chunky mixtures of tomatoes, tomatillos, or fruit, combined with vinegar or citrus juice, chiles, onions, garlic, and cilantro. Our sauces—smoother than the salsas—fall into two groups. One type is used before or during cooking (barbecue sauce, for example); the other sauces are more like relishes, spooned onto foods after cooking.

SALSA FRESCA

This is the most basic salsa in the Southwestern kitchen. Spoon it on cheese appetizers, chili, tamales, scrambled eggs, grilled meat, fish, or poultry.

In a bowl, stir together 3 large ripe **tomatoes**, diced; ½ cup chopped **fresh cilantro** (coriander); and 1 small **onion**, chopped. Season to taste with 5 to 7 tablespoons **fresh jalapeño or other small hot chiles**, stemmed, seeded, and minced; 3 to 4 tablespoons **lime juice**; and **salt.** If made ahead, cover and refrigerate for up to 2 days. Makes about 3½ cups.

TOMATILLO SALSA

Serve this tart green salsa with chiles rellenos, egg dishes, fish, or chicken.

Remove husks and stems from ½ pound **tomatillos** (about 8 medium-size). Coarsely chop tomatillos, then combine with 2 **fresh jalapeño or other small hot chiles**, stemmed, seeded, and minced; 3 tablespoons minced **fresh cilantro** (coriander); 2 tablespoons **lime juice**; and 1 clove **garlic**, minced or pressed. Season to taste with **salt.** If made ahead, cover and refrigerate until next day. Makes about 1½ cups.

GREEN CILANTRO SALSA

Spoon this refreshing mixture on clams or other shellfish, or on grilled lamb or beef.

In a bowl, mix 1 small **onion**, finely chopped; 1 cup chopped **fresh cilantro** (coriander); ½ cup chopped **parsley**; ½ cup **olive oil** or salad oil; 6 tablespoons **lime juice**; 3 tablespoons **distilled white vinegar**; 2 cloves **garlic**, minced or pressed; and 1 **fresh jalapeño or other small hot chile**, stemmed, seeded, and minced. If made ahead, cover and refrigerate until next day. Makes about 2½ cups.

CRANBERRY SALSA

Serve this salsa with Grilled Turkey, Southwest Style (page 61) or other poultry, lamb, or pork dishes.

Cut peel and all white membrane from 2 large **oranges**; lift out sections. Coarsely chop orange sections. Using a knife or a food processor, coarsely chop 2 cups **fresh cranberries.**

In a bowl, combine chopped oranges, cranberries, 4 teaspoons grated **orange peel**, ¼ cup *each* minced **onion** and **salad oil**, 1 tablespoon *each* minced **fresh cilantro** (coriander) and **fresh ginger**, and 1 **fresh jalapeño or other small hot chile**, stemmed, seeded, and minced. Mix thoroughly, then season to taste with **salt.** If made ahead, cover and refrigerate for up to 2 days. Makes about 3 cups.

CITRUS SALSA

Serve this tangy mixture with grilled fish or poultry.

Cut peel and all white membrane from 2 large **oranges** and 1 large **grapefruit**; lift out sections. Coarsely chop fruit. Also peel, core, and chop 2 medium-size **tomatoes.**

In a bowl, mix oranges, grapefruit, tomatoes, 2 tablespoons *each* **lime juice** and **orange juice**, ¼ cup chopped **fresh cilantro** (coriander), and 1 teaspoon **sugar.** Season to taste with **salt.** If made ahead, cover and refrigerate until next day. Makes 3 cups.

BLENDER SALSA

Use this smooth-textured salsa just like Salsa Fresca.

In a blender or food processor, combine 2 medium-size **tomatoes,** cut into chunks; ½ small **onion;** 3 tablespoons **canned diced green chiles;** 4 teaspoons **distilled white vinegar;** and 1 tablespoon chopped **fresh cilantro** (coriander). Whirl until puréed; season to taste with **salt.** If made ahead, cover and refrigerate for up to 2 days. Makes about 2½ cups.

RED CHILE SAUCE

Use this sauce alone on an omelet or as a base for other Southwestern sauces.

Arrange 3 ounces (about 9) **dried red New Mexico or California chiles** on a 12- by 15-inch baking sheet. Bake in a 300° oven until chiles smell toasted (about 4 minutes). Let cool slightly. Discard stems and seeds.

In a 3- to 4-quart pan, combine chiles, 2½ cups **water,** 1 small **onion,** cut into chunks, and 2 cloves **garlic.** Cover and bring to a boil over high heat. Reduce heat; simmer until chiles are very soft when pierced (about 30 minutes). Remove from heat and let cool slightly.

Pour chile mixture into a blender and whirl until very smoothly puréed. Rub purée firmly through a wire strainer to extract all pulp; discard residue. Season purée to taste with **salt.** If made ahead, cover and refrigerate for up to 1 week (freeze for longer storage). Makes about 3 cups.

SMOKY CHIPOTLE BARBECUE SAUCE

Smoked jalapeños give this sauce its fiery flavor. Spoon it on spareribs or other meats while grilling.

Finely chop 5 to 8 **canned chipotle chiles in adobo sauce** (see page 7); set aside.

Heat 3 tablespoons **salad oil** in a 3- to 4-quart pan over medium heat. Add 1 medium-size **onion,** chopped, and 2 cloves **garlic,** minced or pressed. Cook, stirring occasionally, until onion is soft (about 10 minutes). Stir in 1 large can (28 oz.) **tomatoes,** ¼ cup *each* firmly packed **brown sugar** and **red wine vinegar,** and chiles. Break up tomatoes with a spoon, then cover and cook, stirring occasionally, until sauce is thickened and smooth (about 30 minutes). Season to taste with **salt.** If made ahead, cover and refrigerate for up to 10 days. Makes about 3 cups.

SOUTHWEST BARBECUE SAUCE

Brush this smoky, all-purpose sauce on chicken or beef while grilling.

Heat 2 tablespoons **salad oil** in a 3- to 4-quart pan over medium heat. Add 1 medium-size **onion,** chopped, and 1 large clove **garlic,** minced or pressed. Cook, stirring occasionally, until onion is soft (about 10 minutes). Stir in 1 large can (28 oz.) **tomato purée,** ½ cup firmly packed **brown sugar,** ¼ cup **cider vinegar,** 3 tablespoons **Worcestershire,** 2 teaspoons **liquid smoke,** and 1 teaspoon **dry mustard.** Then add 4 to 6 teaspoons **ground New Mexico chile** (see page 7) and 1 to 1½ teaspoons **salt.** Bring to a boil over high heat, then reduce heat, cover, and simmer for 20 minutes to blend flavors. If made ahead, cover and refrigerate for up to 10 days. Makes about 5 cups.

CHILE HOLLANDAISE

Use this sauce to make Southwestern-style Eggs Benedict, or spoon it on grilled fish.

Place 1 large (5- to 6-inch) **dried red New Mexico or California chile** in a 9-inch square baking pan; bake in a 300° oven until chile smells toasted (about 4 minutes). Let cool slightly. Discard stem and seeds. Crumble chile into small pieces.

In a blender, combine chile pieces, 1 tablespoon **hot water,** ½ teaspoon **ground cumin,** 2 teaspoons **lemon juice,** and 1 **egg yolk;** whirl until smoothly puréed. With blender on high speed, slowly add ½ cup (¼ lb.) melted **butter** or margarine in a slow, steady stream, whirling until well blended. Use hot or at room temperature. Makes ¾ cup.

JALAPEÑO MAYONNAISE

Dollop this zippy sauce on grilled fish or poultry, or spread it on sandwiches.

In a blender or food processor, combine 3 or 4 **fresh jalapeño or other small hot chiles,** stemmed, seeded, and minced; 1 clove **garlic,** minced or pressed; 1 large **egg yolk;** 2 tablespoons **lime juice;** and ½ teaspoon **salt.** Whirl until smoothly puréed. With motor running, slowly add ¾ cup **salad oil,** a drop at a time first, then in a slow stream, until all oil is added and mixture is very thick. Cover and refrigerate for at least 1 hour or up to 3 days before serving. Makes about 1 cup.

FLAT BLUE ENCHILADAS

Preparation time: About 2¾ hours
Cooking time: 15 minutes for tortillas; 5 minutes to bake enchiladas

Blue corn tortillas, layered with full-flavored Red Chile Pork Sauce, make up these individual-size enchilada stacks. Crown each stack with a soft-fried egg.

>   Red Chile Pork Sauce (page 34)
>   Salad oil
> 12 Blue Corn Tortillas (page 79) or
>   purchased corn tortillas (6- to 7-inch-
>   diameter)
> 1 small onion, chopped
> 1½ cups (6 oz.) shredded jack cheese
> 1½ cups (6 oz.) shredded Cheddar cheese
> 4 soft-fried eggs (optional)
> 2 cups shredded lettuce
>   Fresh cilantro (coriander) sprigs

Prepare Red Chile Pork Sauce; set aside.

In an 8- to 10-inch frying pan, heat ½ inch oil over medium-high heat. When oil is hot, add 1 tortilla at a time and cook, turning once, just until limp (about 20 seconds *total* for blue tortillas, 10 seconds *total* for regular corn tortillas). Drain on paper towels.

Reheat Red Chile Pork Sauce, if necessary. Lightly coat centers of 4 ovenproof dinner plates with sauce. Place a tortilla over sauce on each plate and sprinkle with a little onion and some shredded cheese; then top with a spoonful of sauce. Repeat, making 2 more layers on each plate (use all Red Chile Pork Sauce, onions, and cheese). Place plates in a 350° oven until cheese is melted (about 5 minutes). Top each stack with an egg, if desired. Garnish with lettuce and cilantro. Makes 4 servings.

Per serving: 771 calories, 30 g protein, 52 g carbohydrates, 52 g total fat, 97 mg cholesterol, 717 mg sodium

TOMATILLO CHICKEN ENCHILADAS

Pictured on facing page

Preparation time: About 45 minutes
Cooking time: About 10 minutes for tortillas; 15 to 30 minutes to bake enchiladas

Green tomatillos blended with green chiles and cilantro make the tart, green-green sauce for these hearty chicken enchiladas.

>   Tomatillo Sauce (recipe follows)
> 4 cups coarsely shredded cooked chicken
>   or turkey
> 3 cups (12 oz.) shredded jack cheese
> 1 can (7 oz.) diced green chiles
> 1½ teaspoons dry oregano leaves
>   Salt
>   Salad oil
> 12 corn tortillas (6- to 7-inch-diameter)
> 1 to 1½ cups sour cream
> ½   cup chopped fresh cilantro (coriander) or
>   fresh cilantro (coriander) sprigs
> 1 or 2 tomatillos, husked and thinly sliced;
>   or 1 lime, thinly sliced

Prepare Tomatillo Sauce; set aside.

In a large bowl, mix chicken, 2 cups of the cheese, chiles, and oregano. Season to taste with salt; set aside.

In an 8- to 10-inch frying pan, heat ½ inch oil over medium-high heat. When oil is hot, add 1 tortilla at a time; cook, turning once, just until limp (about 10 seconds *total*). Drain on paper towels.

While tortillas are warm, spoon ½ cup chicken mixture down center of each; roll to enclose. Set enchiladas, seam side down, in a 10- by 15-inch baking pan. (At this point, you may cover and refrigerate until next day.)

Cover enchiladas with foil and bake in a 350° oven until hot in center (about 15 minutes; 30 minutes if refrigerated). Uncover and top with remaining 1 cup cheese. Bake, uncovered, until cheese is melted (about 10 more minutes).

Meanwhile, reheat Tomatillo Sauce. To serve, spoon Tomatillo Sauce onto a large rimmed platter (or divide among 6 dinner plates). Set enchiladas on sauce. Spoon sour cream down center of enchiladas, sprinkle with cilantro, and garnish with tomatillo slices. Makes 6 servings.

TOMATILLO SAUCE. Heat ⅓ cup **salad oil** in a 3- to 4-quart pan over medium-high heat. Add 2 medium-size **onions,** chopped; cook, stirring often, until soft (about 10 minutes). Stir in 1 can (7 oz.) **diced green chiles;** 2 cans (13 oz. *each*) **tomatillos,** drained; 1 cup **regular-strength chicken broth;** 3 tablespoons **lime juice;** 2 teaspoons *each* **dry oregano leaves** and **sugar;** and 1 teaspoon **ground cumin.** Bring to a boil; then reduce heat and simmer, uncovered, stirring occasionally, for 25 minutes. Whirl sauce in a blender or food processor until smooth. Season to taste with **salt.**

Per serving: 873 calories, 50 g protein, 40 g carbohydrates, 58 g total fat, 158 mg cholesterol, 1,057 mg sodium

Bathed in smooth, piquant green sauce, these Tomatillo Chicken Enchiladas
(recipe on facing page) are topped with melted jack cheese and sour cream.
Garnish each serving with fresh cilantro and a few thin tomatillo slices.

43

MAIN DISHES

MEATS, POULTRY, FISH, EGGS & CHEESE

Throughout the Southwest, today's cooks delight in serving their bountiful supply of fresh foods with a new, lighter flair, while preserving the ancient foundations of their sometimes fiery cuisine.

This combination of innovation and tradition is particularly evident in Southwestern entrées. Barbecued beef and pork continue to be popular, with fajitas and pork ribs jockeying for top honors—but now they are joined on the grill by newer creations such as Chili-basted Chicken with Pineapple Salsa and Grilled Birds with Jalapeño Jelly Glaze.

Slow simmering is still a favorite way to cook the less tender cuts of meat. Shredded and sauced, they're often tucked into warm flour tortillas, then topped with shredded lettuce and cheese for a satisfying meal. New Mexican Beef Brisket and Carne Adobada are two new versions we suggest.

Evidence of the lighter trend is the increase in whole-meal salads, served hot or chilled. Nogales Baked Chicken, reminiscent of a tostada, and Chile Shrimp & Corn Salad are just two examples.

Throughout the region, egg and cheese dishes are longtime favorites for breakfast, brunch, or supper. True to the Southwest's heritage, chiles are frequently included, as in our Casserole Quiche and Red Chile & Cheese Omelet.

Fajitas

Pictured on front cover

Preparation time: 30 to 40 minutes
Marinating time: 4 hours or until next day
Grilling time: 15 to 20 minutes

Along the Mexican border, *fajitas* (fa-HEE-tas) means skirt steaks. Elsewhere, however, the word has become a catchall term for make-it-yourself burritos filled with grilled meat.

3	**pounds skirt steak, trimmed of excess fat**
½	**cup lime juice**
⅓	**cup salad oil**
⅓	**cup tequila or lime juice**
4	**cloves garlic, minced or pressed**
1½	**teaspoons ground cumin**
1	**teaspoon dry oregano leaves**
½	**teaspoon pepper**
4	**or 5 small onions (unpeeled), cut in half lengthwise**
3	**cans (about 1 lb. *each*) refried beans**
	Salsa Fresca (page 40)
	Guacamole (page 16)
8	**to 10 green onions, rinsed well and drained**
16	**to 20 flour tortillas (about 8-inch-diameter)**
	Sour cream
	Fresh cilantro (coriander) sprigs

Cut steak crosswise into about 12-inch lengths, then arrange in a 9- by 13-inch dish. In a small bowl, stir together lime juice, oil, tequila, garlic, cumin, oregano, and pepper. Pour over meat; turn meat to coat. Place onion halves, cut side down, in marinade alongside meat. Cover and refrigerate for at least 4 hours or until next day, turning meat occasionally.

Place beans in a large pan and heat through; keep warm. Meanwhile, prepare Salsa Fresca and Guacamole; set aside.

Place onion halves on a lightly greased grill 4 to 6 inches above a solid bed of hot coals. Cook for about 7 minutes; turn over. Lift meat from marinade and drain briefly (reserve marinade). Place on grill. Tie green onions together with string 3 inches from roots to form a brush. Baste meat and onion halves with marinade, using green onion brush. Continue to cook onion halves until soft and browned (5 to 9 more minutes). Cook meat, turning once, until browned and done to your liking; cut to test (about 6 minutes for rare).

Transfer cooked meat and onions to a carving board; keep warm. Roll green onion brush in marinade and lay on grill; turn often until tops are wilted (3 to 5 minutes). Place brush on board; remove string. Thinly slice meat across the grain.

Heat tortillas on grill as needed, turning often with tongs, just until softened (15 to 30 seconds). Place a few meat slices down center of each tortilla; top with some beans, a few pieces of onion from onion halves, Salsa Fresca, Guacamole, sour cream, and cilantro. Fold up bottom, then fold in sides to enclose. Eat green onions alongside. Makes 8 to 10 servings.

Per serving: 615 calories, 40 g protein, 61 g carbohydrates, 24 g total fat, 70 mg cholesterol, 575 mg sodium

Barbecued Beef Short Ribs

Preparation time: About 20 minutes, plus 40 minutes for Red Chile Sauce
Marinating time: 4 hours or until next day
Grilling time: 30 to 40 minutes

From northern New Mexico comes this recipe for meaty beef ribs soaked in a mild chile-seasoned marinade, then grilled in a covered barbecue.

6	**pounds lean, meaty beef short ribs, cut into serving-size pieces**
½	**cup Red Chile Sauce (page 41)**
1½	**cups dry red wine**
3	**tablespoons olive oil**
1	**small onion, chopped**
2	**cloves garlic, minced or pressed**
½	**teaspoon *each* salt and pepper**
1	**dry bay leaf**
1	**tablespoon unseasoned meat tenderizer**

Place meat in a large, heavy plastic bag. Prepare Red Chile Sauce, then stir in wine, oil, onion, garlic, salt, pepper, and bay leaf. Pour over meat and seal bag. Refrigerate for 4 hours or until next day, turning bag over several times.

Drain and reserve marinade. Following package directions, sprinkle meat with tenderizer and pierce all over with a fork.

Place meat on a lightly greased grill 4 to 6 inches above a solid bed of medium coals. Put lid on barbecue, drafts open (or cover with a tent of heavy-duty foil). Cook, turning and basting occasionally with marinade, until meat near bone is done to your liking; cut to test (30 to 40 minutes for medium-rare). Makes 6 servings.

Per serving: 1,141 calories, 49 g protein, 4 g carbohydrates, 102 g total fat, 212 mg cholesterol, 1,306 mg sodium

Tender slices of New Mexican Beef Brisket (recipe on facing page) topped with a spicy chile sauce are ready to be tucked into warm flour tortillas, along with sharp cheese and shredded lettuce. Roll up to eat out of hand.

NEW MEXICAN BEEF BRISKET

Pictured on facing page

Preparation time: 30 to 35 minutes
Marinating time: 24 hours
Baking time: 6 hours

Slowly simmered and sauced brisket is a popular entrée throughout the Southwest. In parts of Texas this dish is referred to as "que," even though it's baked instead of grilled.

> 3½- to 4-pound beef brisket, trimmed of excess fat
> 2 teaspoons celery salt
> 4 cloves garlic, minced or pressed
> 2 teaspoons coarsely ground black pepper
> 1 teaspoon liquid smoke
> ⅓ cup Worcestershire
> 4 ounces dried red New Mexico or California chiles
> 2 cups boiling water
> 1 tablespoon salad oil
> 2 tablespoons all-purpose flour
> ½ teaspoon *each* ground cumin and dry oregano leaves
> Salt
> 1 medium-size onion, thinly sliced
> 10 to 12 warm flour tortillas (about 8-inch-diameter)
> Shredded lettuce
> Shredded sharp Cheddar cheese

Place meat in a large, heavy plastic bag. In a small bowl, combine celery salt, 2 cloves of the garlic, pepper, liquid smoke, and Worcestershire. Pour over meat and seal bag. Refrigerate for 24 hours, turning bag over several times.

Remove meat and place on a piece of heavy-duty foil, 18 by 25 inches. Pour marinade over meat and seal foil. Place in a 10- by 15-inch baking pan. Bake in a 300° oven for 5 hours.

Meanwhile, remove and discard stems and seeds from chiles. Place chiles in a bowl and pour boiling water over them; let stand until soft (about 20 minutes). In a blender, whirl chiles and about half the soaking liquid (reserve remainder) to make a thick purée. Set aside.

In a 2-quart pan, heat oil over medium heat; add flour and stir until lightly browned. Stir in remaining 2 cloves garlic, cumin, and oregano. Place a wire strainer over pan. Add puréed chiles, forcing them through with the back of a spoon; add remaining soaking liquid to help force purée through. Cook, stirring, until bubbly. Season to taste with salt.

Remove brisket from oven. Carefully drain liquid; reserve and refrigerate. Spoon chile mixture over meat; top with onion. Reseal foil; continue to bake until meat is tender when pierced (1 more hour).

Lift brisket from foil and cut across the grain into ¼-inch-thick slices. Drain chile sauce into a pan. Discard solidified fat from chilled marinade; add marinade to chile sauce and heat over medium heat. Serve meat and sauce in tortillas; pass lettuce and cheese to top individual servings. Makes 10 to 12 servings.

Per serving: 308 calories, 25 g protein, 26 g carbohydrates, 12 g total fat, 62 mg cholesterol, 395 mg sodium

BARBACOA

Preparation time: About 40 minutes
Marinating time: 2 to 3 hours
Baking time: 2½ to 3 hours

The flavor secret of this oven-baked beef roast is a seasoning paste you make by grinding whole spices with dried mild and hot chiles.

> José's Seasoning (recipe follows)
> 5-pound bone-in beef chuck roast or 6- to 6½-pound leg of lamb, boned and cut into chunks
> Salt
> 3 tablespoons white wine vinegar
> Salsa Fresca (page 40)

Prepare José's Seasoning; set aside. Sprinkle meat with salt and vinegar; cover and refrigerate for 2 to 3 hours.

Drain meat and place in a 5- to 6-quart pan. Spread seasoning over meat. Cover and bake in a 350° oven until very tender when pierced (2½ to 3 hours). Meanwhile, prepare Salsa Fresca; cover and refrigerate. To serve, lift meat from pan and cut or tear into shreds. Pass salsa to spoon over meat. Makes 6 to 8 servings.

JOSÉ'S SEASONING. Discard stems and seeds from 4 **dried red New Mexico or California chiles**, 2 **dried ancho chiles**, 2 **small dried hot red chiles**, and 2 **dried cascabel chiles** (or 1 more small dried hot red chile). Tear or break chiles into pieces. Cover with ½ cup **hot water** and let stand until soft (about 20 minutes); drain. In a blender, combine drained chiles, 10 cloves **garlic**, 1 tablespoon **dry oregano leaves**, 2 teaspoons *each* **whole cloves** and **cumin seeds**, 1 teaspoon **cracked black pepper**, ½ teaspoon **ground cinnamon**, and ½ can (13-oz. size) **tomatillos** (drained). Whirl until chiles are finely chopped.

Per serving: 667 calories, 49 g protein, 10 g carbohydrates, 48 g total fat, 171 mg cholesterol, 109 mg sodium

Flank Steak Santa Fe

Preparation time: About 30 minutes
Baking time: About 1¾ hours

Chorizo sausage sparks the stuffing for this oven-simmered flank steak. Bake some carrots and onions at the same time for an easy oven meal.

- 3 chorizo sausages (about ¾ lb. *total*), casings removed
- 1½ cups unseasoned croutons
- ⅓ cup *each* chopped green onions (including tops) and parsley
- 2 eggs, lightly beaten
- 1½- to 2-pound flank steak
- 3 tablespoons salad oil
- 1 jar (12 oz.) green chile salsa

Crumble sausage into a wide frying pan. Cook over medium heat, stirring, until meat is browned; then drain off fat. Remove from heat and stir in croutons, onions, parsley, and eggs.

Butterfly steak by slicing in half horizontally almost all the way through. Spread open and pound to ¼-inch thickness. Spoon chorizo mixture over half the steak; fold ends in, roll to enclose, and tie securely with string.

Heat oil in frying pan over medium-high heat; add meat and brown evenly on all sides. Transfer to an ungreased 2-quart baking dish and pour salsa over all. Cover and bake in a 375° oven until meat is tender when pierced (about 1¾ hours). Remove string. Skim and discard fat, then spoon sauce over meat. Makes about 6 servings.

Per serving: 733 calories, 44 g protein, 42 g carbohydrates, 42 g total fat, 192 mg cholesterol, 1,346 mg sodium

Tucson Taco Salad

Preparation time: 20 to 30 minutes

Now you can enjoy tacos in neat-to-eat salad form. Combine traditional taco makings in a bowl; then add tortilla chips as a stand-in for taco shells.

- 1 pound lean ground beef
- 1 large onion, chopped
- 1 tablespoon chili powder
- ½ teaspoon *each* ground cumin and dry oregano leaves
- Purchased taco sauce

- 1 medium-size head iceberg lettuce, shredded
- 1 cup thinly sliced green onions (including tops)
- 1 small cucumber, peeled, seeded, and diced
- 1½ cups (6 oz.) shredded sharp Cheddar cheese
- 3 cups crushed tortilla or corn chips
- 2 medium-size tomatoes, cut into wedges
- Sour cream

Crumble beef into a wide frying pan. Cook over medium-high heat, stirring, until browned. Stir in chopped onion and cook, stirring often, until soft (about 10 minutes); discard excess fat. Add chili powder, cumin, oregano, and 2 to 3 tablespoons taco sauce; mix well.

Place lettuce in a large salad bowl. Add green onions, cucumber, and cheese. Add meat mixture and tortilla chips; mix well. Garnish with tomatoes.

Pass sour cream and additional taco sauce at the table. Makes 6 to 8 servings.

Per serving: 393 calories, 19 g protein, 29 g carbohydrates, 23 g total fat, 57 mg cholesterol, 398 mg sodium

Cal-Mex Burgers

Preparation time: 10 to 15 minutes
Grilling time: 10 to 12 minutes

Jack cheese, green chiles, and pinto beans hide inside these barbecued hamburgers. Serve them in warm flour tortillas with complementary toppings.

- 1½ pounds lean ground beef
- 1 medium-size white onion, chopped
- 6 slices (1 oz. *each*) jack cheese
- ¼ cup canned diced green chiles
- ¼ cup canned pinto beans, drained
- Salt and pepper
- Butter or margarine
- 6 flour tortillas (about 8-inch-diameter)
- Purchased taco sauce
- Fresh cilantro (coriander) sprigs
- Thinly sliced tomatoes

Mix beef and onion together, then divide into 6 equal portions and shape each into a patty about 6 inches in diameter. Cut cheese slices diagonally in half to make triangles. Arrange 1 triangle on half of each meat patty so tips of cheese touch edges of meat. Evenly spoon chiles over cheese, then evenly top with beans and sprinkle with salt and pepper. Arrange remaining cheese triangles on top. Fold plain half of meat patty over filling and pinch edges together to seal, forming a half moon of stuffed meat.

Place patties on a lightly greased grill 4 to 6 inches above a solid bed of hot coals. Cook, turning as needed to brown both sides, until meat in center is done to your liking; cut to test (10 to 12 minutes for medium-rare).

Meanwhile, lightly butter tortillas. Stack, wrap in foil, and place at side of grill to warm. Turn package over several times to heat evenly.

To serve, place stuffed meat patty on a tortilla and top with taco sauce, cilantro, and tomatoes; then fold tortilla in half to eat out of hand. Makes 6 servings.

Per serving: 449 calories, 30 g protein, 20 g carbohydrates, 27 g total fat, 100 mg cholesterol, 268 mg sodium

BEEF TONGUE IN CHIPOTLE SAUCE

Preparation time: 20 to 30 minutes
Cooking time: About 3½ hours

Canned chipotle chiles, sold either pickled *(en escabeche)* or in adobo sauce, are readily available in Mexican markets. If you can't find them, use our easy-to-make substitute.

> 3- to 3½-pound fresh, smoked, or corned **beef tongue**
>
> 2 tablespoons **salad oil**
>
> 2 large **onions,** sliced
>
> 2 cloves **garlic,** minced or pressed
>
> 1 large can (28 oz.) **tomatoes**
>
> ½ teaspoon *each* ground **cumin, salt,** and **pepper**
>
> ½ to 1 can (7-oz. size) pickled **chipotle chiles,** or Chipotle Chiles Substitute (recipe follows)
>
> 1 small green **bell pepper,** seeded and cut into thin rings

Place tongue in a 5- to 6-quart pan; cover with cold water. Bring to a boil over high heat; then reduce heat, cover, and simmer until tender when pierced (about 3 hours). Let cool. Remove skin; trim off roots and excess fat. Thinly slice tongue. Set aside.

Heat oil in a wide frying pan over medium heat; add onions and garlic. Cook, stirring often, until onions are soft (about 10 minutes). Meanwhile, in a blender, combine tomatoes and their liquid, cumin, salt, pepper, and chipotle chiles and their sauce. Whirl until smooth. Add to onions and bring to a simmer. Add sliced tongue, cover, and simmer until hot through (about 25 minutes).

Transfer meat and sauce to a rimmed platter. Garnish with bell pepper. Makes 6 to 8 servings.

CHIPOTLE CHILES SUBSTITUTE. Combine 1½ to 2 tablespoons firmly packed **brown sugar,** ¼ cup **distilled white vinegar,** 1 teaspoon *each* paprika and **sesame oil,** 1 to 1½ teaspoons **crushed red pepper,** ½ teaspoon **hickory-flavored salt,** and ¼ teaspoon **liquid smoke.**

Per serving: 447 calories, 27 g protein, 15 g carbohydrates, 31 g total fat, 145 mg cholesterol, 778 mg sodium

ROAST LAMB WITH CHILE RICE & VEGETABLES

Preparation time: About 20 minutes
Roasting time: About 1½ hours

A word of warning: Just one jalapeño chile produces mildly hot rice. You can adjust the amount to suit your own tolerance for chile "fire."

> 5- to 5½-pound **leg of lamb**
>
> 3 tablespoons **olive oil**
>
> 1½ teaspoons **cumin seeds**
>
> 1½ cups thinly sliced **green onions** (including tops)
>
> 1 cup **rice**
>
> 2 large **carrots,** diced
>
> 2 large thin-skinned **potatoes,** peeled and diced
>
> 1 or 2 fresh or canned **jalapeño chiles,** stemmed, seeded, and minced
>
> 3 cups regular-strength **chicken broth**

Rub lamb with 1 tablespoon of the oil and 1 teaspoon of the cumin seeds. Set lamb on a rack in a shallow roasting pan. Roast in a 350° oven until a meat thermometer inserted in thickest part of meat (not touching bone) registers 140°F (about 1½ hours).

Meanwhile, in a 5- to 6-quart pan, combine remaining 2 tablespoons oil, onions, and rice. Stir over medium-high heat until onions are soft (about 10 minutes). Stir in remaining ½ teaspoon cumin seeds, carrots, potatoes, chiles, and broth. Bring to a boil over high heat; then reduce heat, cover, and simmer until potatoes are tender when pierced (25 to 30 minutes).

Transfer lamb to a serving board. Skim and discard fat from pan juices; stir juices into rice. Serve rice alongside lamb. Makes 6 to 8 servings.

Per serving: 492 calories, 49 g protein, 34 g carbohydrates, 17 g total fat, 156 mg cholesterol, 442 mg sodium

Roasted Salsa Spareribs

Pictured on facing page

Preparation time: About 20 minutes
Grilling time: About 1½ hours

The barbecue does double duty when you prepare these succulent pork ribs. Start by charring tomatoes and green chiles for a piquant salsa; then grill the ribs, using the salsa as a basting sauce.

    6   large, firm-ripe tomatoes
    8   large fresh mild green chiles such as
        Anaheim
    ¼   cup *each* red wine vinegar and chopped
        fresh cilantro (coriander)
    3   cloves garlic, minced or pressed
        Salt
    6   to 8 pounds pork spareribs
        Lime slices (optional)
        About 1 cup sour cream
    3   or 4 limes, cut into wedges

To prepare fire, mound and ignite 50 charcoal briquets. When coals are heavily spotted with gray ash, spread to make an even layer.

Set tomatoes and chiles on a lightly greased grill 4 to 6 inches above prepared coals. Cook, turning as needed, until chiles are charred on all sides (7 to 10 minutes) and tomatoes are hot and streaked with brown (about 15 minutes).

Using long tongs, mound hot charcoal for barbecuing by indirect heat (see page 56), adding 5 fresh briquets to each side.

To make the salsa, chop grilled tomatoes and chiles; discard stems and seeds. Place tomatoes and chiles and their juices in a bowl. Stir in vinegar, cilantro, and garlic; season to taste with salt. Spread some of the salsa evenly over both sides of ribs.

Place ribs, meat side up, on grill directly above drip pan (overlap ribs to fit on grill if necessary). Cover barbecue and adjust dampers as necessary to maintain an even heat. Cook, basting occasionally with some of the remaining salsa, until meat near bone is no longer pink; cut to test (1 to 1¼ hours).

To serve, cut ribs into 2- to 3-rib portions; garnish with lime slices, if desired. Pass remaining salsa, sour cream, and lime wedges at the table. To eat, top ribs with salsa, sour cream, and a squeeze of lime. Makes 6 to 8 servings.

Per serving: 721 calories, 52 g protein, 4 g carbohydrates, 54 g total fat, 214 mg cholesterol, 168 mg sodium

Pork with Chocolate Mint Sauce

Preparation time: About 30 minutes
Baking time: About 1 hour

Echoing the spirit of a Mexican *mole* sauce, a small amount of unsweetened chocolate gives rich flavor, deep color, and luxurious texture to this complex sauce for sliced pork loin.

        3-pound boneless pork loin roast
    3   tablespoons olive oil or salad oil
        About ⅓ cup water
    1   large carrot, chopped
    1   stalk celery, chopped
    1   small onion, chopped
    ½   cup blanched almonds
    2   to 3 tablespoons chopped fresh
        mint leaves
    2   cloves garlic
    1½ ounces unsweetened chocolate
    3   to 4 tablespoons balsamic vinegar or
        red wine vinegar
    3   tablespoons sugar
    ¼   cup raisins
    ¼   cup pine nuts or slivered almonds

Trim and discard excess fat from pork. Heat 1 tablespoon of the oil in a wide frying pan over medium-high heat; add pork and cook, turning as needed, until browned on all sides. Transfer pork to a 7- by 11-inch baking pan. Add ⅓ cup water to frying pan and scrape up browned bits; pour over pork. Add remaining 2 tablespoons oil, carrot, celery, and onion to frying pan. Stir over medium heat until vegetables are soft; add vegetables to pork.

Cover meat and bake in a 350° oven until meat is no longer pink in center; cut to test (about 1 hour).

Meanwhile, in a food processor or blender, whirl blanched almonds, mint, and garlic until finely ground. Set aside.

When pork is done, remove from pan and keep warm. Pour pan juices and vegetables through a wire strainer set over a large measuring cup; discard vegetables. Add water to juices to make 1 cup, or boil juices, uncovered, to reduce to 1 cup. Pour juices into frying pan; place over low heat. Add chocolate and stir until melted. Add mint mixture, vinegar, sugar, raisins, and pine nuts; stir until sauce thickens to the texture of whipping cream.

Thinly slice pork; offer sauce to spoon over individual servings. Makes 6 to 8 servings.

Per serving: 368 calories, 30 g protein, 9 g carbohydrates, 25 g total fat, 78 mg cholesterol, 90 mg sodium

Juicy Roasted Salsa Spareribs (recipe on facing page) are paired with corn on the cob for this casual barbecue dinner. Grilled tomatoes and mild green chiles are the foundation of the basting sauce; you might grill a few extra to serve alongside the ribs.

Carne Adobada

Preparation time: 30 to 40 minutes
Marinating time: 1 to 2 days
Baking time: About 2½ hours

Serve this northern New Mexico specialty in warm flour tortillas, topped with Green Chile Cream Sauce and cheese.

- 10 **to 12 dried red New Mexico or California chiles (3 to 4 oz. *total*)**
     About 2 cups water
- 2 **cloves garlic, minced or pressed**
- 1 **teaspoon *each* salt and dry oregano leaves**
- 3 **pounds lean boneless pork butt or shoulder**
     Green Chile Cream Sauce (recipe follows)
- 4 **tablespoons butter or margarine**
- 12 **flour tortillas (about 8-inch-diameter)**
- 1 **cup (4 oz.) shredded Cheddar cheese**

Lay chiles in a 10- by 15-inch baking pan and place in a 300° oven until aromatic (about 4 minutes). Let cool, then remove and discard stems, seeds, and veins.

In a 2½- to 3-quart pan, combine chiles and 2 cups water. Cover and simmer gently until chiles are very soft (about 20 minutes).

In a blender or food processor, whirl chiles and water until puréed. Using the back of a spoon, force purée through a wire strainer; discard residue. Stir garlic, salt, and oregano into chile purée. Measure and add water, if needed, to make 1½ to 1¾ cups; set aside.

Trim and discard excess fat from meat. Cut meat into ¼-inch-thick slices, then cut into strips about ¾ inch wide and 3 inches long. Combine meat and chile purée; cover and refrigerate for 1 to 2 days.

Transfer meat and purée to a 4- to 5-quart pan. Cover tightly and bake in a 325° oven until meat is very tender when pierced (about 2½ hours). Skim and discard fat; keep meat warm.

Prepare Green Chile Cream Sauce; set aside. Melt 2 tablespoons of the butter in a wide frying pan over medium heat. Turn 1 tortilla in butter, then lay flat and spoon 1/12 of the meat mixture down center. Roll to enclose; set, seam side down, in a 9- by 13-inch baking pan. Repeat to fill remaining tortillas, melting remaining 2 tablespoons butter as needed. Top rolled tortillas evenly with Green Chile Cream Sauce and cheese. Broil 4 to 6 inches below heat just until cheese is melted (about 1 minute). Makes 6 servings.

GREEN CHILE CREAM SAUCE. In a 2-quart pan, melt ¼ cup **butter** or margarine over medium heat. Add ¼ cup **all-purpose flour** and cook, stirring, until bubbly. Stir in 1 cup *each* **half-and-half** and **regular-strength chicken broth.** Cook, stirring, until sauce boils and thickens. Stir in 2 to 3 tablespoons **canned diced green chiles.**

Per serving: 850 calories, 51 g protein, 42 g carbohydrates, 54 g total fat, 207 mg cholesterol, 1,008 mg sodium

Pork & Yams in Spicy Orange Sauce

Preparation time: 20 to 30 minutes
Cooking time: About 40 minutes

Fresh oranges and pork are paired in a number of dishes throughout the Southwest. Here, juicy pork shoulder chops simmer with sweet potatoes in a spicy-hot orange sauce.

- 1 **tablespoon salad oil**
- 6 **pork shoulder chops (about 2¼ lbs. *total*), cut about ¾ inch thick**
- 1 **large onion, chopped**
- 2 **cloves garlic, minced or pressed**
- 1 **beef bouillon cube dissolved in ½ cup boiling water**
- 1½ **cups orange juice**
- ½ **teaspoon *each* crushed red pepper, ground cumin, and dry oregano leaves**
- 1 **large can (26 oz.) yam halves, drained**
- 1 **tablespoon lemon juice**
- 2 **teaspoons cornstarch**
- 1 **teaspoon grated orange peel**
- 2 **tablespoons chopped fresh cilantro (coriander) or parsley**
- 1 **medium-size orange, peeled and thinly sliced**

Heat oil in a wide frying pan over medium-high heat; add pork chops and cook until browned on both sides, then set aside. Add onion and garlic to pan and cook, stirring often, until onion is soft (about 10 minutes). Stir in bouillon, orange juice, pepper, cumin, and oregano; return chops to pan. Bring to a boil over high heat; then reduce heat, cover, and simmer until pork is tender when pierced (about 40 minutes). Arrange yams in pan with chops during last 5 minutes. Transfer chops and yams to a platter; keep warm.

Blend together lemon juice, cornstarch, and orange peel. Stir into pan drippings and cook, stirring, until sauce boils and thickens. Spoon sauce over meat and yams. Sprinkle with cilantro and garnish with orange slices. Makes 6 servings.

Per serving: 545 calories, 24 g protein, 38 g carbohydrates, 33 g total fat, 94 mg cholesterol, 290 mg sodium

STEAMED PORK IN BANANA LEAVES

——

Soaking time for achiote seeds: 12 hours
Preparation time: 20 to 30 minutes
Marinating time: 8 hours or until next day
Baking time: 3 to 3½ hours

To make this unusual entrée, you enclose a seasoned pork roast in banana leaves, ti leaves, or foil, then oven-steam it. Look for refrigerated or frozen banana leaves in Mexican or Southeast Asian markets. Ti leaves can be purchased from a florist.

 ⅔ **cup Achiote Paste (page 55)**
  3½- to 4-pound boneless pork shoulder
  Prepared banana leaf or leaves (directions follow); or 6 ti leaves (stems removed); or foil, cut or arranged to make a 12- by 20-inch rectangle
 8 **to 10 flour tortillas (about 8-inch-diameter)**
  Salsa Fresca (page 40)

Prepare Achiote Paste; set aside. Score fat side of pork with ½-inch-deep cuts. Position meat in center of banana leaf, ti leaves, or foil. Spread Achiote Paste over roast; rub into cuts. Fold leaf or foil to enclose; tie securely with string. Refrigerate for at least 8 hours or until next day.

Place a rack in bottom of a deep 6- to 8-quart pan; pour in 1½ cups water and set wrapped roast on rack. Cover and bake in a 350° oven until roast is very tender when pierced through leaves (3 to 3½ hours). Add more hot water if necessary. Stack tortillas, wrap in foil, and heat alongside pork during last 15 minutes. Also prepare Salsa Fresca.

To serve, place roast on a board. Slit packet open lengthwise on top; peel back leaf. Pour pan juices over meat (if you used foil, discard juices). Let guests pull off pieces of pork to pile on flour tortillas and top with salsa. Makes 8 to 10 servings.

PREPARED BANANA LEAVES. Buy 1 package (about 1 lb.) **refrigerated or frozen banana leaves;** thaw if frozen (you can refreeze extra leaves).

Thoroughly rinse leaves and pat dry. Glide flat surface of leaves across gas flame or electric element (on high) of your range; in a few seconds, leaves will become shiny and more flexible. Set aside.

Per serving: 617 calories, 33 g protein, 22 g carbohydrates, 44 g total fat, 131 mg cholesterol, 345 mg sodium

CHILI PORK STEAKS

——

Preparation time: 15 to 20 minutes
Marinating time: 2 hours or until next day
Cooking time: About 10 minutes

For a delicious flavor contrast, serve these chili-spiked pork steaks with a cool salad of cucumber and oranges.

 4 **pork shoulder steaks (about 6 oz. *each*), cut ½ inch thick**
 1½ **tablespoons chili powder**
 1 **teaspoon *each* dry oregano leaves and garlic salt**
 ¼ **teaspoon ground cumin**
 3 **tablespoons wine vinegar**
 3 **tablespoons salad oil**
  Green Chile Salsa (recipe follows)
 ¾ **cup Guacamole (page 16)**
 ¾ **cup sour cream**

Trim and discard excess fat from steaks; set steaks aside. In a small bowl, combine chili powder, oregano, garlic salt, cumin, vinegar, and 1 tablespoon of the oil. Rub mixture on both sides of pork steaks. Cover and refrigerate for at least 2 hours or until next day. Meanwhile, prepare Green Chile Salsa and Guacamole; cover and refrigerate.

Heat remaining 2 tablespoons oil in a wide frying pan over medium-high heat. Add pork steaks and cook until pork is no longer pink in thickest part; cut to test (about 5 minutes per side).

Serve pork with Green Chile Salsa, Guacamole, and sour cream. Makes 4 servings.

GREEN CHILE SALSA. Combine 1 large **tomato,** chopped; 1 small **onion,** chopped; 1 can (4 oz.) **diced green chiles;** and 1 tablespoon **vinegar.**

Per serving: 522 calories, 28 g protein, 15 g carbohydrates, 40 g total fat, 102 mg cholesterol, 817 mg sodium

Individual banana leaf packets hold Chicken with Achiote (recipe on facing page).
Topped with thick onion and tomato slices and bathed in a flavorful sauce,
this Mexican-inspired entrée is served with plantains and fresh fruit.

CHICKEN WITH ACHIOTE

Pictured on facing page

Soaking time for achiote seeds: 12 hours
Preparation time: 20 to 30 minutes
Marinating time: 8 hours or until next day
Baking time: 1¾ to 2 hours

Mellow achiote paste seasons these oven-steamed chicken quarters. Tuck sweet potatoes into the same oven for a no-fuss feast.

5½ tablespoons Achiote Paste (recipe follows)
2 tablespoons salad oil
1 large onion, cut into ½-inch-thick slices
2 large tomatoes, cut into ½-inch-thick slices
  3½- to 4-pound frying chicken, cut into quarters
4 prepared banana leaf sections, *each* 12 by 15 inches (page 53); or 8 ti leaves (stems removed); or 4 sheets foil, *each* 12 by 15 inches
¼ cup boiling water

Prepare Achiote Paste; set aside. Heat oil in a wide frying pan over medium heat; add onion and cook, turning, until soft. Add tomatoes and 1½ tablespoons of the Achiote Paste; cook, turning gently, until tomatoes are soft (1 to 2 minutes).

Rinse chicken; pat dry. Using tip of a sharp knife, deeply pierce chicken all over. Rub 1 tablespoon of the Achiote Paste on each quarter, then place each on a banana leaf and top with ¼ of the tomato mixture.

Fold leaves around chicken; tie securely with string. Refrigerate for at least 8 hours or until next day.

Arrange bundles in a 9- by 13-inch baking dish; pour in water. Cover and bake in a 300° oven until chicken is tender when pierced through leaves (1½ to 1¾ hours). Slit leaf packet on top and peel back leaves. Increase oven temperature to 450° and continue baking chicken, uncovered, until topping is browned (about 10 more minutes). Makes 4 servings.

ACHIOTE PASTE. Place 2 ounces (⅓ cup) **achiote (annatto) seeds** in a bowl with **boiling water** to cover; cover tightly and let stand for 12 hours to soften.

Drain seeds; discard liquid. Combine seeds in a blender with 1 tablespoon **ground cumin**, 1 teaspoon **coarsely ground black pepper**, 2 teaspoons **ground allspice**, 2 tablespoons chopped **garlic**, 2 **small dried hot red chiles** (torn in pieces), 1½ teaspoons **salt**, and 6 tablespoons *each* **orange juice** and **white wine vinegar.** Whirl until smooth; it takes several minutes. Use, or cover and refrigerate

for up to 10 days (freeze for longer storage). Makes about 1 cup.

Per serving: 781 calories, 60 g protein, 12 g carbohydrates, 55 g total fat, 232 mg cholesterol, 511 mg sodium

CHICKEN IN ESCABECHE SAUCE

Preparation time: 20 to 25 minutes
Cooking time: About 1 hour

Garlic, pepper, sweet spices, and herbs make a potent seasoning paste for chicken. After baking, you quickly grill the chicken pieces to crisp and brown the skin.

2½ tablespoons Escabeche Paste (recipe follows)
  3½- to 4-pound frying chicken, cut up
1½ cups regular-strength chicken broth
1 tablespoon salad oil
2 large onions, thinly sliced
1 can (7 oz.) diced green chiles
1½ tablespoons cornstarch mixed with 1½ tablespoons water
3 tablespoons chopped fresh cilantro (coriander)

Prepare Escabeche Paste. Rinse chicken; pat dry. Using tip of a sharp knife, pierce chicken all over. Rub paste all over chicken, pushing some under skin. Place chicken in a 9- by 13-inch baking pan; pour in broth. Cover and bake in a 400° oven until chicken is tender when pierced (about 40 minutes).

Lift chicken from broth; drain briefly. Skim and discard fat from broth; reserve broth. Place chicken on a lightly greased grill 4 to 6 inches above a solid bed of medium coals. Cook, turning as needed, until well browned (10 to 15 minutes).

Meanwhile, heat oil in a wide frying pan over medium heat; add onions and cook, stirring, until soft (about 10 minutes). Stir in chiles, reserved broth, and cornstarch mixture. Cook, stirring, until sauce boils and thickens. Stir in cilantro. Spoon sauce onto individual portions of chicken. Makes 4 or 5 servings.

ESCABECHE PASTE. Stir together 8 cloves **garlic,** minced or pressed; 1 teaspoon *each* **ground allspice, ground cloves, ground cumin,** and **ground coriander;** 1½ teaspoons **ground cinnamon;** ¾ teaspoon **coarsely ground pepper;** 2 teaspoons **dry oregano leaves;** ¼ teaspoon **ground red pepper** (cayenne); and 2 tablespoons *each* **orange juice** and **white wine vinegar.** Use, or cover and refrigerate for up to 2 weeks. Makes ¼ cup.

Per serving: 471 calories, 47 g protein, 12 g carbohydrates, 25 g total fat, 141 mg cholesterol, 611 mg sodium

Barbecuing Basics

Both regular charcoal briquets and mesquite charcoal are good fuels for grilling. Mesquite charcoal is gaining in popularity nationwide; many home and restaurant chefs claim that it burns hotter than regular charcoal and gives foods a smokier flavor. In our tests, we've found that mesquite does burn hotter, but it doesn't always noticeably enhance flavor: though mesquite-grilled fish and poultry do take on a more intensely smoky taste, beef and pork gain little additional flavor.

Mesquite coals aren't uniformly shaped; they range in size from tiny shards to 4-inch chunks. The fire will be hotter where large lumps jut upward, so break up big pieces for more even heat.

Fire Temperature

Three different terms are commonly used to indicate desired fire temperature.

- **Hot** describes coals that are barely covered with gray ash. You can hold your hand near the grill for only 2 to 3 seconds.

- **Medium** describes coals that glow through a layer of gray ash. You can hold your hand near the grill for only 4 to 5 seconds.

- **Low** describes coals covered with a thick layer of gray ash. You should be able to hold your hand near the grill for 6 to 7 seconds.

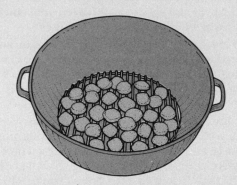

Barbecuing by Direct Heat

Suitable for burgers, chops, steaks, poultry pieces, and other fairly small foods. Open the bottom dampers if your barbecue has them. Spread briquets on the fire grate in a solid layer that's 1 to 2 inches bigger all around than the grill area required for the food. Then mound the charcoal and ignite it. When the coals have reached the fire temperature specified in the recipe, spread them out into a single layer again.

Set grill in place at the recommended height above coals. Grease grill lightly, then arrange food on grill. Watch carefully and turn as needed to ensure even cooking. If you're using a baste that's high in sugar or fat, apply it during the last part of cooking and turn food often to prevent scorching. Use a water-filled spray bottle to extinguish flare-ups.

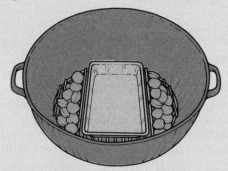

Barbecuing by Indirect Heat

Suitable for whole fish as well as roasts, whole poultry, and other food that requires long cooking. Open or remove lid from a covered barbecue; open bottom dampers. Pile 50 long-burning briquets on fire grate and ignite. Let burn until hot (about 30 minutes). Using long-handled tongs, bank half the briquets on each side of grate; place a metal drip pan in center.

Set grill in place 4 to 6 inches above pan; lightly grease grill. Set food on grill directly above drip pan. If you're grilling meat, place it fat side up (drain marinated meat briefly before placing it on grill). Cover barbecue and adjust dampers as necessary to maintain an even heat. Add 5 or 6 briquets to each side of grate at 30- to 40-minute intervals as needed to keep fire temperature constant.

Nogales Baked Chicken

Preparation time: About 15 minutes
*Baking time: About 35 minutes for breasts;
about 45 minutes for thighs*

These oven-fried chicken parts, served on a bed of lettuce and topped with yogurt, green onions, tomatoes, and avocado, will remind you of tostadas. Offer Crispfried Tortilla Pieces (page 77) alongside.

3 **whole chicken breasts (about 1 lb.** *each*),
**skinned, boned, and split; or 12 chicken
thighs (3 to 3½ lbs.** *total***), skinned**

2 **eggs**

1 **clove garlic, minced or pressed**
Purchased green chile salsa or taco sauce

1½ **cups fine dry bread crumbs**

2 **teaspoons** *each* **chili powder and ground
cumin**

½ **teaspoon ground oregano**

6 **tablespoons butter or margarine**

1 **large ripe avocado**

4 **to 6 cups shredded iceberg lettuce**
About 1 cup plain yogurt or sour cream
**About 6 tablespoons thinly sliced green
onions (including tops)**

12 **to 18 cherry tomatoes**

1 **or 2 limes, cut into wedges**
Salt

Rinse chicken and pat dry. Set aside.

In a shallow bowl, beat together eggs, garlic, and ¼ cup salsa. In another shallow bowl, combine bread crumbs, chili powder, cumin, and oregano. Dip 1 chicken piece in egg mixture to coat; drain briefly, then coat in crumb mixture. Shake off excess. Repeat with remaining chicken pieces.

Melt butter in a rimmed 10- by 15-inch baking pan in a 375° oven. Add chicken; turn to coat with butter. Bake, uncovered, until meat in thickest part is no longer pink; cut to test (30 to 35 minutes for breasts, about 45 minutes for thighs).

Pit, peel, and slice avocado. Arrange chicken on a bed of shredded lettuce and top each piece with a dollop of yogurt. Garnish with avocado, onions, tomatoes, and lime wedges; offer additional yogurt and salsa. Season chicken to taste with salt. Makes 6 servings.

Per serving: 508 calories, 43 g protein, 31 g carbohydrates, 24 g total fat, 211 mg cholesterol, 538 mg sodium

Chicken, Corn & Onion Salad

Preparation time: 35 to 40 minutes
Cooking time: About 30 minutes

For a light approach, try this hot shredded chicken salad offered on poached onion halves, with cilantro-dressed corn on the cob alongside.

3 **large onions, cut in half crosswise
and peeled**

3 **ears fresh or frozen corn, cut into
2-inch pieces**
Hot Tomato Sauce (recipe follows)

3 **cups cooked, shredded chicken**
Cilantro Dressing (recipe follows)
Fresh cilantro (coriander) sprigs
Salt and pepper

In a 5- to 6-quart pan, bring 2 to 3 quarts water to a boil. Add onions, reduce heat, cover, and simmer until tender when pierced (about 20 minutes). With a slotted spoon, lift onions from water; handling gently, turn upside down to drain. Set aside. Return water to boiling; add corn. Cook, uncovered, just until corn is hot (about 5 minutes); drain and set aside.

Prepare Hot Tomato Sauce; mix in chicken and cook over medium-high heat, stirring often, until chicken is heated through (about 5 minutes). Also prepare Cilantro Dressing.

To serve, place onions, cut side up, on 6 dinner plates. Mound hot chicken salad equally onto each onion half. Place corn alongside and drizzle with Cilantro Dressing. Garnish with cilantro sprigs. Season to taste with salt and pepper and pass remaining dressing to spoon over individual portions. Makes 6 servings.

Hot Tomato Sauce. Heat 2 tablespoons **olive oil** in a wide frying pan over medium-high heat; add 1 small **onion,** minced, and 2 cloves **garlic,** minced or pressed. Cook, stirring often, until onion is soft (about 10 minutes). Add 2 small **fresh jalapeño chiles,** seeded and minced, and 4 large **tomatoes,** peeled and chopped. Boil, uncovered, stirring often, until liquid from tomatoes evaporates (about 15 minutes). Stir in ⅓ cup chopped **fresh cilantro** (coriander).

Per serving: 268 calories, 24 g protein, 21 g carbohydrates, 11 g total fat, 62 mg cholesterol, 78 mg sodium

Cilantro Dressing. Combine ½ cup **salad oil,** ⅓ cup chopped **fresh cilantro** (coriander), and ¼ cup **lime juice.** Makes about 1 cup.

Per tablespoon: 61 calories, 0 g protein, .25 g carbohydrates, 7 g total fat, 0 mg cholesterol, .7 mg sodium

CHILI-BASTED CHICKEN WITH PINEAPPLE SALSA

Preparation time: About 25 minutes
Grilling time: 40 to 50 minutes

Chile lovers will enjoy this chicken. There's chili powder and cayenne pepper in the baste; liquid hot pepper seasoning heats up the fresh Pineapple Salsa served alongside the meat.

- 2 frying chickens (about 3½ lbs. *each*)
- 1 teaspoon *each* chili powder and paprika
- ¼ teaspoon ground red pepper (cayenne)
- 2 tablespoons salad oil
- 2 teaspoons Dijon mustard
  Pineapple Salsa (recipe follows)

Remove chicken necks and giblets; reserve for other uses, if desired. Discard lumps of fat. With poultry shears or a knife, cut through each chicken along both sides of backbone. Discard backbones. Place each chicken, skin side up, on a flat surface and press firmly, cracking breastbone slightly, until bird lies reasonably flat. Rinse and pat dry.

In a small bowl, smoothly blend chili powder, paprika, red pepper, oil, and mustard. Brush evenly over chicken skin.

Place chickens, skin side up, on a lightly greased grill 4 to 6 inches above a solid bed of medium coals. Put lid on barbecue, drafts open (or cover with a tent of heavy-duty foil). Cook until meat near thighbone is no longer pink; cut to test (40 to 50 minutes).

Meanwhile, prepare Pineapple Salsa. To serve, cut each chicken into quarters; offer salsa on the side. Makes 8 servings.

Per serving: 452 calories, 48 g protein, .54 g carbohydrates, 27 g total fat, 154 mg cholesterol, 184 mg sodium

PINEAPPLE SALSA. Cut top from 1 small **pineapple** (about 3 lbs.). With a grapefruit knife, cut fruit from shell in chunks. Reserve shell and top. Coarsely chop pineapple and place in a colander to drain; save juice to drink. In a bowl, stir together drained pineapple; 1 medium-size mild **red onion,** minced; ¾ cup finely chopped **fresh cilantro** (coriander); 1 tablespoon **white wine vinegar;** and ½ teaspoon **liquid hot pepper seasoning.** Spoon salsa into pineapple shell; present top alongside. Makes about 3½ cups.

Per tablespoon: 7 calories, .05 g protein, 2 g carbohydrates, .05 g total fat, 0 mg cholesterol, 1 mg sodium

GRILLED BIRDS WITH JALAPEÑO JELLY GLAZE

Pictured on facing page

Preparation time: 15 to 20 minutes
Grilling time: 7 to 40 minutes, depending on type of bird

A spicy-sweet glaze adds a lively dimension to grilled game hens or quail. You'll find the jalapeño jelly for the glaze in specialty food stores and some well-stocked supermarkets.

To accompany the crisp-skinned birds, you might serve a selection of other grilled foods you can eat out of hand: corn on the cob, crusty garlic bread, or warmed flour tortillas. Tomatillo, Jicama & Apple Salad (page 16) and Marinated Bell Pepper Strips (page 74) are two other choices.

- 6 to 8 Rock Cornish game hens
    (1¼ to 1½ lbs. *each*) or 18 to 24 quail
    (2½ to 4 oz. *each*), thawed if frozen
- ¼ cup butter or margarine
- ⅔ cup jalapeño jelly
- 2 tablespoons lime juice
  Salt and pepper
  Lime wedges (optional)

Remove poultry necks and giblets; reserve for other uses, if desired. If using game hens, cut in half. If using quail, cut through backbone of each bird with poultry shears or a knife. Place quail, skin side up, on a flat surface and press firmly, cracking bones slightly, until birds lie flat. Rinse poultry and pat dry.

In a pan, combine butter and jelly. Stir over medium heat until melted. Stir in lime juice; set aside. Place birds, skin side up, on a lightly greased grill 4 to 6 inches above a solid bed of medium coals (for game hen) or hot coals (for quail).

Cook game hens until meat near thighbone is no longer pink; cut to test (30 to 40 minutes). Turn several times during cooking; during last 15 minutes, baste often with jelly mixture.

Cook quail until skin is browned and breast meat is cooked through, but still pink near bone; cut to test (7 to 8 minutes). Turn several times during cooking; during last 5 minutes, baste often with jelly mixture.

Sprinkle birds lightly with salt and pepper before serving; garnish with lime wedges, if desired. Makes 6 to 8 servings.

Per serving: 785 calories, 75 g protein, 19 g carbohydrates, 43 g total fat, 259 mg cholesterol, 292 mg sodium

Plump, glistening Grilled Birds with Jalapeño Jelly Glaze (recipe on facing page) make
an impressive main dish that belies its quick and easy preparation. Cilantro Slaw (page 74) and
fresh pineapple wedges complement the succulent game hen halves.

Quail with Chipotle Chiles

Preparation time: About 30 minutes
Baking time: About 7 minutes

Canned chipotle chiles, chicken broth, and sour cream make a speedy, distinctive sauce for these tiny birds.

    8   corn tortillas (6- to 7-inch-diameter), cut
        into ⅛-inch-wide strips
   12   quail (2½ to 4 oz. *each*), thawed if frozen
    1   tablespoon salad oil
    2   tablespoons canned chipotle chiles in
        adobo sauce, minced
   ½   cup regular-strength chicken broth
        About ¾ cup sour cream
        Sliced green onions (including tops)
        Salt

Fry tortilla strips as for Crisp Tortilla Strips (page 31); set aside.

Rinse quail and pat dry. Pour oil into a wide frying pan with an ovenproof handle. Heat over high heat. Fill pan with birds, without crowding. Lightly brown on all sides, turning as needed (3 to 4 minutes). Pile all browned quail into frying pan and place in a 500° oven until birds are hot (about 7 minutes); centers of breasts should be pink to red (cut to test). Set aside.

Divide shoestring tortillas equally among 4 dinner plates. In a small bowl, stir together chiles, broth, and ½ cup of the sour cream. Spoon about 2 tablespoons of the sauce on each plate. Set 3 birds in sauce; spoon a dollop of sour cream on the side. Garnish with onions. Accompany with remaining sauce. Dip birds and tortillas in sauce as you eat them with your fingers; season to taste with salt. Makes 4 servings.

Per serving: 848 calories, 66 g protein, 28 g carbohydrates, 52 g total fat, 19 mg cholesterol, 440 mg sodium

Duck with Citrus-Chile Marinade

Preparation time: About 15 minutes
Marinating time: 6 hours or until next day
Grilling time: About 2 hours

Use one duck or two for this recipe, depending on the number of servings you need. (Expect plenty of sauce if you cook just one duck.)

    1   or 2 ducks (4½ to 5 lbs. *each*),
        thawed if frozen
   ⅓   cup sugar
   1½   cups orange juice
   ¾   cup lime juice
   ½   to 1 teaspoon crushed dried hot red
        chiles
    1   tablespoon *each* grated orange peel and
        lime peel
    1   tablespoon *each* cornstarch and water

Remove duck neck and giblets; reserve for other uses, if desired. Discard lumps of fat. Rinse duck inside and out and pat dry.

Place duck in a large, heavy plastic bag. In a small bowl, combine sugar, orange juice, lime juice, chiles, orange peel, and lime peel. Stir until sugar is dissolved. Pour over duck and seal bag. Place bag in a shallow baking pan. Refrigerate for at least 6 hours or until next day, turning bag over several times.

Lift duck from marinade and drain briefly (reserve marinade). Fasten neck skin to back with a small metal skewer. Barbecue duck by indirect heat (see page 56), placing duck, breast up, on grill directly above drip pan. Cover barbecue and adjust dampers as necessary to maintain an even heat. Cook for 1¼ hours; then baste with marinade. Continue to cook, basting frequently, until meat near bone at hip socket is no longer pink; cut to test (about 45 more minutes).

Transfer duck to a platter and keep warm. In a 2-quart pan, combine cornstarch and water; stir in remaining marinade and bring to a boil over high heat, stirring constantly. Pour into a serving bowl and pass at the table to spoon over individual portions. Makes 3 to 6 servings.

Per serving: 1,012 calories, 55 g protein, 11 g carbohydrates, 82 g total fat, 242 mg cholesterol, 173 mg sodium

Turkey with Chocolate Orange Sauce

Preparation time: About 15 minutes
Cooking time: About 10 minutes

Southwestern cooks frequently borrow ideas from their Mexican neighbors. Here, it's a sauce secret: unsweetened chocolate.

    2   pounds boned turkey breast, cut into
        ¼-inch-thick slices
        All-purpose flour
   ½   cup (¼ lb.) butter or margarine

About ¼ cup salad oil
¾ cup dry Marsala wine or regular-strength chicken broth
1 tablespoon finely shredded orange peel
¼ cup orange juice
1 ounce unsweetened chocolate
2 tablespoons sugar
Thin orange slices
Salt

Place turkey slices between sheets of plastic wrap and gently pound with a flat-surfaced mallet to an even ⅛-inch thickness. (At this point, you may cover and refrigerate until next day.)

Coat turkey with flour; shake off excess. In a wide frying pan over medium-high heat, combine 1 tablespoon of the butter and 1 tablespoon of the oil. When butter begins to foam, add turkey in a single layer. Cook until lightly browned on both sides (about 1½ minutes *total*); remove from pan and keep warm. Repeat to cook remaining turkey, adding more butter and oil as needed.

Add Marsala, orange peel, orange juice, chocolate, and sugar to pan. Cook over low heat, stirring, until chocolate is melted. Add all remaining butter; stir constantly until butter is melted and incorporated into sauce. Pour over turkey. Garnish with orange slices. Season to taste with salt. Makes 6 to 8 servings.

Per serving: 324 calories, 27 g protein, 4 g carbohydrates, 22 g total fat, 101 mg cholesterol, 195 mg sodium

GRILLED TURKEY, SOUTHWEST STYLE

Pictured on page 11

Preparation time: 5 to 10 minutes
Grilling time: 1½ to 2 hours

Sweet Potatoes with Tequila & Lime (page 69) and Roasted Cheese-stuffed Chiles (page 71) go well with this barbecued turkey. You might begin the meal with Antojitos Tray (page 16).

10- to 12-pound turkey, thawed if frozen
About 4 limes, cut in half
About 4 teaspoons dry oregano leaves
Salt and pepper

Remove turkey neck and giblets; reserve for other uses, if desired. Discard large lumps of fat. Rinse and pat dry.

Before cooking, squeeze 1 or 2 lime halves and rub over turkey and inside cavities; sprinkle with oregano, then lightly sprinkle with salt and pepper inside and out.

Barbecue turkey by indirect heat (see page 56), placing turkey, breast up, on grill directly above drip pan. Cover barbecue and adjust dampers as necessary to maintain an even heat. Cook turkey until a meat thermometer inserted in thickest part of thigh (not touching bone) registers 185°F or until meat near thighbone is no longer pink (cut to test)—about 3 hours. Every 30 minutes, squeeze 1 or 2 lime halves and rub over turkey.

Transfer turkey to a platter. To carve, cut off wings and slice breast. Cut off legs and slice meat from thighs. Makes about 12 servings.

Per serving: 348 calories, 60 g protein, 1 g carbohydrates, 9 g total fat, 157 mg cholesterol, 152 mg sodium

BARBECUED RABBIT

Preparation time: About 5 minutes
Marinating time: 1 hour or until next day
Grilling time: About 35 minutes

Mild-flavored, fine-textured rabbit tastes much like chicken—and like chicken, it takes well to grilling.

3- to 3½-pound frying rabbit, cut up
Paprika Marinade (recipe follows)

Rinse rabbit pieces and pat dry. Arrange in a single layer in a shallow dish. Prepare Paprika Marinade; pour over rabbit. Cover and refrigerate for at least 1 hour or until next day, turning occasionally.

Lift rabbit from marinade and drain briefly (reserve marinade). Barbecue rabbit by indirect heat (see page 56), placing rabbit on grill directly above drip pan. Cover barbecue and adjust dampers as necessary to maintain an even heat. Cook, basting often with marinade, until meat is white at bone; cut to test (about 35 minutes). Makes 4 or 5 servings.

PAPRIKA MARINADE. In a bowl, stir together ½ cup **salad oil**, ¼ cup **red wine vinegar**, 2 tablespoons **paprika**, 1 tablespoon **Worcestershire**, and 1 clove **garlic**, minced or pressed.

Per serving: 549 calories, 54 g protein, 3 g carbohydrates, 35 g total fat, 165 mg cholesterol, 145 mg sodium

A pair of toppings—creamy Jalapeño Mayonnaise (page 41) and Citrus Salsa (page 40)—
enhance Barbecued Trout (recipe on facing page).
Garnish the fish with grilled green onions and orange slices, if you like.

BARBECUED TROUT

Pictured on facing page

Preparation time: About 30 minutes
Marinating time: 1 to 2 hours
Grilling time: 6 to 8 minutes

Before grilling, these tender trout soak up flavor in an herbed marinade. Serve with Citrus Salsa and Jalapeño Mayonnaise or the Nut Butter.

> 4 **whole trout (about ½ lb. *each*), cleaned**
> ⅔ **cup salad oil**
> ¼ **cup white wine vinegar**
> ½ **teaspoon *each* dry basil and dry oregano leaves**
> 1 **clove garlic, minced or pressed**
> ¼ **teaspoon *each* salt and pepper**
> **Citrus Salsa (page 40) and Jalapeño Mayonnaise (page 41); or Nut Butter (recipe follows)**

Rinse fish, pat dry. Leave whole or bone and butterfly.

To bone cleaned trout and keep head and tail in place, open body cavity; insert a sharp knife at head end under backbone and cut between ribs and flesh. Repeat process to free other side. Cut underneath backbone to free. Using kitchen scissors, snip backbone at head and tail; lift out and discard. Cut off and discard fins. Spread fish out flat.

In a shallow pan, stir together oil, vinegar, basil, oregano, garlic, salt, and pepper. Add fish to oil mixture; turn to coat. Cover and refrigerate for 1 to 2 hours, turning once. Meanwhile, prepare Citrus Salsa and Jalapeño Mayonnaise; cover and refrigerate. Or prepare Nut Butter and keep warm.

Lift fish from marinade and drain briefly (discard marinade). Barbecue whole fish by indirect heat (see page 56), placing fish on grill directly above drip pan. Place boned fish on a well-greased grill 4 to 6 inches above a solid bed of hot coals.

Cook whole or boned fish, turning once, just until fish flakes when prodded with a fork in thickest part (10 to 12 minutes for whole fish, 6 to 8 minutes for boned fish). With a wide metal spatula, transfer cooked trout to a warm rimmed platter. Accompany with Citrus Salsa and Jalapeño Mayonnaise, or drizzle with Nut Butter. Makes 4 servings.

Per serving: 440 calories, 21 g protein, 1 g carbohydrates, 39 g total fat, 55 mg cholesterol, 190 mg sodium

NUT BUTTER. In a small pan, combine ¼ cup **butter** or margarine and ½ cup **pine nuts** or chopped pecans. Cook over medium heat, stirring, until butter is melted; keep warm.

Per tablespoon: 194 calories, 4 g protein, 3 g carbohydrates, 21 g total fat, 31 mg cholesterol, 118 mg sodium

TEX-MEX RED SNAPPER

Preparation time: About 30 minutes
Baking time: About 45 minutes

Whole red snapper baked in a cinnamon- and clove-accented fresh tomato sauce makes an impressive entrée. Pimento-stuffed olives and cilantro garnish the platter.

> 2 **tablespoons olive oil or salad oil**
> 1 **large onion, chopped**
> 2 **cloves garlic, minced or pressed**
> 4 **teaspoons sugar**
> 1 **teaspoon salt**
> ¼ **teaspoon *each* ground cinnamon and ground cloves**
> 5 **cups peeled, seeded, chopped tomatoes**
> 1½ **teaspoons *each* lemon juice and water**
> 1 **tablespoon cornstarch**
> 1 **or 2 fresh or canned jalapeño chiles, seeded and finely chopped**
> 2 **tablespoons capers, drained**
> **5- to 5½-pound cleaned and scaled whole red snapper or other rockfish, head removed**
> ⅓ **cup thinly sliced pimento-stuffed green olives**
> 3 **tablespoons finely chopped fresh cilantro (coriander)**

Heat oil in a wide frying pan over medium heat; add onion and garlic and cook, stirring often, until onion is soft (about 10 minutes). Stir in sugar, salt, cinnamon, cloves, and tomatoes. Cook, stirring, over high heat until a thick sauce forms (about 8 minutes).

Blend together lemon juice, water, and cornstarch; stir into tomato mixture. Cook until mixture boils and turns clear; remove from heat. Stir in chiles and capers.

Rinse fish and pat dry. Place a 24-inch sheet of foil crosswise in a large roasting pan. Grease foil lightly, then place fish on foil; pour hot tomato sauce over fish. Bake, uncovered, in a 400° oven until fish flakes when prodded with a fork in thickest part (about 45 minutes). Baste frequently with sauce during last 15 minutes of baking.

Skim watery juices off sauce with a spoon; then stir sauce to blend. Lift foil, fish, and clinging sauce and slide onto a platter; drizzle with remaining sauce in pan. Garnish with olives and cilantro.

To serve, cut fish to bone, then lift off each serving. Makes 4 to 6 servings.

Per serving: 306 calories, 45 g protein, 13 g carbohydrates, 8 g total fat, 119 mg cholesterol, 819 mg sodium

CHILE SHRIMP & CORN SALAD

Preparation time: 30 to 40 minutes
Chilling time: 1 to 4 hours

Combining shrimp with such regional basics as chiles and corn is another example of the exciting, ever-developing cuisine of the Southwest.

> 3 small dried hot red chiles
> ¼ cup olive oil or salad oil
> ½ teaspoon pepper
> 2 cups corn kernels, cut from 2 large ears corn; or 1 package (10 oz.) frozen corn kernels, thawed and drained
> 1 medium-size red bell pepper, seeded and diced
> 1½ pounds medium-size shrimp, shelled and deveined
> 1 tablespoon soy sauce
> ⅔ cup cider vinegar
> About 1 pound spinach
> About 1 pound green leaf lettuce

In a wide frying pan over medium heat, combine chiles and oil; cook, stirring, until chiles are lightly browned (about 4 minutes). Add pepper, corn, and bell pepper. Cook over high heat, stirring constantly, until vegetables are tender to bite (about 3 more minutes). Add shrimp; stir just until they turn light pink (about 3 minutes).

Remove pan from heat. Stir in soy sauce and vinegar, then spoon mixture into a bowl. Let cool, then cover and refrigerate until shrimp are cold (at least 1 hour or up to 4 hours).

Meanwhile, discard spinach stems; wash leaves and pat dry. Also wash lettuce leaves and pat dry. Place in plastic bags and refrigerate until serving time.

To serve, tear greens into bite-size pieces; place in a large salad bowl, then spoon shrimp mixture over top. Use chiles as garnish or remove and discard. Mix salad and serve. Makes about 6 servings.

Per serving: 255 calories, 24 g protein, 17 g carbohydrates, 11 g total fat, 131 mg cholesterol, 425 mg sodium

CHILLED FISH IN ESCABECHE

Preparation time: About 30 minutes
Chilling time: 8 hours or until next day

The same spicy paste that seasons baked-grilled chicken acts as the marinade and dressing for this light but satisfying warm weather entrée.

> 4 teaspoons Escabeche Paste (page 55)
> ⅓ cup olive oil or salad oil
> 2 cloves garlic, minced or pressed
> ⅓ cup *each* orange juice and white wine vinegar
> ⅔ cup regular-strength chicken broth
> 2 teaspoons sugar
> 2 dry bay leaves
> About 2 pounds fish fillets such as red snapper, lingcod, or sole; or 2 pounds 1-inch-thick pieces of swordfish, halibut, or shark
> 1 large mild red onion, sliced and separated into rings
> 1 can (4 oz.) whole green chiles, drained and seeded
> Spinach leaves
> ½ cup fresh cilantro (coriander) leaves

Prepare Escabeche Paste. Heat 1 tablespoon of the oil in a 2- to 3-quart pan over medium heat; add Escabeche Paste and garlic. Cook, stirring, for 1 minute. Gradually stir in orange juice, vinegar, broth, sugar, and bay leaves; bring to a boil over high heat. Then reduce heat and keep warm.

Fold thin fish fillets in half to form 1-inch-thick pieces. Heat 3 more tablespoons oil in a wide frying pan over medium heat. Add fish in a single layer; cook, turning once, until fish is golden brown on outside and flakes when prodded with a fork (4 to 5 minutes per side). Repeat to cook remaining fish, adding more oil as needed.

Arrange fish in a 9-inch square baking dish; top with onion. Spoon warm escabeche mixture over fish. Cover and refrigerate for at least 8 hours or until next day; spoon marinade over fish several times.

Lay chiles flat on a rimmed platter; surround with spinach. Set fish on chiles; top with onion and cilantro. Spoon marinade over all. Makes 6 to 8 servings.

Per serving: 214 calories, 23 g protein, 6 g carbohydrates, 10 g total fat, 62 mg cholesterol, 231 mg sodium

PUFFY CHILE RELLENO CASSEROLE

Preparation time: About 20 minutes
Baking time: About 40 minutes

You can control the hotness of this soufflé-like casserole by the number of chiles you add. It's a good choice for a weekend brunch.

> 2 or 3 cans (7 oz. *each*) whole green chiles
> 4 corn tortillas (6- to 7-inch-diameter), cut into wide strips

4 cups (1 lb.) shredded jack cheese
1 large tomato, seeded and sliced
8 eggs
½ cup milk
½ teaspoon *each* salt, pepper, ground cumin, and garlic powder
¼ teaspoon onion salt
  Paprika

Remove and discard seeds from chiles; lay half the chiles in bottom of a well-greased 9-inch square baking dish. Top with half the tortilla strips and half the cheese. Arrange tomato slices on top. Repeat layers, using remaining chiles, tortillas, and cheese.

Beat together eggs, milk, salt, pepper, cumin, garlic powder, and onion salt; pour evenly over all and sprinkle lightly with paprika.

Bake, uncovered, in a 350° oven until puffy and set in the center when lightly touched (about 40 minutes). Let stand for about 10 minutes before cutting into squares. Makes 6 to 8 servings.

Per serving: 354 calories, 22 g protein, 13 g carbohydrates, 24 g total fat, 326 mg cholesterol, 912 mg sodium

RED CHILE & CHEESE OMELET

Preparation time: 2 to 3 minutes, plus 40 minutes for Red Chile Sauce
Cooking time: About 2 minutes

A spicy sauce made from dried chiles is a delicious and colorful topping for cheese omelets. A dollop of sour cream mellows each serving.

  Red Chile Sauce (page 41)
2 eggs
1 tablespoon water
1 to 2 teaspoons butter or margarine
1 tablespoon chopped green onion (including top)
2 to 3 tablespoons shredded Cheddar or jack cheese
  Sour cream

Prepare Red Chile Sauce; set aside. In a bowl, beat eggs and water until blended. Heat a 6- or 7-inch omelet pan or other frying pan over medium-high heat. When pan is hot, add butter and stir until it melts. Pour eggs into pan. Cook just until omelet is set but still moist on top; as eggs set, lift cooked portion around edges of pan with a spatula to allow uncooked portion to flow underneath. Remove from heat.

Spoon 1 to 2 tablespoons Red Chile Sauce onto half of omelet; top with onion and cheese. With a spatula,

fold other half of omelet over filling. Slide omelet from pan onto a plate. Offer additional sauce and sour cream to spoon over omelet. Makes 1 serving.

Per serving: 316 calories, 18 g protein, 2 g carbohydrates, 26 g total fat, 591 mg cholesterol, 486 mg sodium

CASSEROLE QUICHE

Preparation time: 20 to 30 minutes
Baking time: 25 to 30 minutes

For a breakfast buffet, you can fry the tortilla chips and prepare the other casserole ingredients a day ahead. Then assemble the casserole just before baking.

6 corn tortillas (6- to 7-inch-diameter)
1 pound lean ground beef
1 large onion, chopped
1 clove garlic, minced or pressed
1 medium-size green bell pepper, seeded and chopped
1 can (7 oz.) green chile salsa
1 teaspoon *each* dry oregano leaves and ground cumin
1 tablespoon chili powder
  Salt
2 cups (8 oz.) shredded sharp Cheddar cheese
1 can (7 oz.) whole green chiles, seeded and cut into strips
6 eggs
1½ cups milk
  Sliced ripe olives

Cut each tortilla into 8 wedges. Prepare as directed for Crisp-fried Tortilla Pieces (page 77); set aside.

Crumble beef into a wide frying pan. Cook over medium heat, stirring occasionally, until meat is browned. Add onion, garlic, and bell pepper; cook for 5 minutes. Stir in salsa, oregano, cumin, and chili powder; season to taste with salt.

Arrange about half the tortilla wedges in a greased shallow 3-quart casserole; top evenly with about half the meat mixture, then half the cheese. Distribute chile strips over cheese. Top with remaining meat mixture and cheese. Tuck remaining tortilla wedges, with points up, around edge of dish. Beat together eggs, milk, and ¼ teaspoon salt; pour over top. Bake in a 375° oven until top feels set when lightly touched (25 to 30 minutes). Garnish with olives. Makes 6 to 8 servings.

Per serving: 427 calories, 25 g protein, 18 g carbohydrates, 28 g total fat, 284 mg cholesterol, 646 mg sodium

Huevos Rancheros

Pictured on facing page

Preparation time: About 30 minutes
Cooking time: About 30 minutes total

There are many versions of this longtime favorite, but the basic ingredients remain the same—eggs, corn tortillas, and a sauce or two.

> **Spiced Tomato Sauce (recipe follows)**
> **Salsa Fresca (page 40)**
> **Fried Tortillas (directions follow)**
> 6 to 12 fried eggs
> **Garnishes (suggestions follow)**

Prepare Spiced Tomato Sauce; keep warm. Prepare Salsa Fresca; cover and refrigerate. Fry tortillas and keep warm.

For each serving, place 1 or 2 tortillas on a plate; top with 1 or 2 fried eggs and about ½ cup sauce. Garnish as desired; accompany with salsa. Makes 6 servings.

SPICED TOMATO SAUCE. Mince 2 large **onions;** seed and mince 1 large **green bell pepper.** In a wide frying pan, heat 3 tablespoons **salad oil;** add onion and bell pepper and cook, stirring often, until soft. Add 1 can (about 14 oz.) **pear-shaped tomatoes** (break up with a spoon) and their liquid, 1 can (14½ oz.) **regular-strength chicken broth,** 1 or 2 cans (10 oz. *each*) **red chile sauce,** and ½ teaspoon *each* **dry oregano leaves** and **cumin seeds.** Boil, uncovered, stirring to prevent sticking, until sauce is reduced to about 3 cups.

FRIED TORTILLAS. You will need 6 to 12 **corn tortillas** (6- to 7-inch-diameter). In an 8- to 10-inch frying pan, heat ½ inch **salad oil** over medium-high heat. When oil is hot, add tortillas, 1 at a time.

For soft-fried tortillas, cook, turning once, just until soft (about 10 seconds *total*). Drain on paper towels.

For crisp-fried tortillas, cook, turning once, until crisp and golden brown (45 to 60 seconds *total*). Drain on paper towels.

GARNISHES. Choose 1 or more of the following: **avocado slices** or Guacamole (page 16), **fresh cilantro** (coriander), **radishes,** shredded **lettuce,** chopped **green onions** (including tops), shredded **jack or Cheddar cheese, lime wedges.**

Per serving (based on 1 egg, 1 tortilla, ½ cup sauce): 263 calories, 9 g protein, 21 g carbohydrates, 15 g total fat, 279 mg cholesterol, 1,114 mg sodium

Eggs with Black Beans & Plantains

Preparation time: About 30 minutes, plus about 2¼ hours for Sopaipillas
Cooking time: 3 to 5 minutes for eggs

Instead of eggs, hashed browns, and sausage, try serving eggs on bacon-flavored refried black beans with puffy Sopaipillas on the side.

> **Sopaipillas (page 82)**
> **Refried Black Beans (recipe follows)**
> **Fried Plantains (recipe follows)**
> 4 to 6 tablespoons butter or margarine
> 8 eggs
> Salt and pepper
> ⅓ cup crumbled *cotija* (Mexican-style dry white cheese) or grated Parmesan cheese
> 4 small limes, halved
> 8 to 16 radishes
> Honey

Prepare Sopaipillas; keep warm. Also prepare Refried Black Beans and Fried Plantains; keep warm.

Melt 2 to 3 tablespoons butter in each of 2 wide frying pans over low heat. Crack 4 eggs into each pan; cook until softly set. Spoon beans equally onto 8 warm dinner plates. Top each with 1 egg; season to taste with salt and pepper. Place Fried Plantains alongside; sprinkle with cheese. Offer lime halves to squeeze over top. Garnish plates with radishes; serve with Sopaipillas and honey. Makes 8 servings.

REFRIED BLACK BEANS. In a 4-quart pan, cook 12 slices (about ¾ lb.) **bacon,** cut into ½-inch-wide pieces, until lightly browned; stir often. Add 2 large **onions,** chopped; cook, stirring often, until soft (about 10 minutes). Drain 4 cans (about 1 lb. *each*) **black beans,** reserving about ½ cup liquid (or use 4 cups cooked dried black beans, page 69). Mash beans with a heavy spoon or potato masher. Cook over low heat, stirring often, until hot throughout. If mixture is dry, add ⅓ to ½ cup reserved bean liquid. Season to taste with **salt.**

FRIED PLANTAINS. Peel 3 large **plantains** (skins will be almost black) or firm, green-tipped bananas. Cut into ¼-inch-thick diagonal slices. In a 4-quart pan, heat about 1 inch **salad oil** to 375°F on a deep-frying thermometer. Drop plantains in oil, about ⅓ at a time. Fry until lightly browned (2 to 3 minutes). Lift from oil and place on a baking sheet lined with paper towels; keep warm in a 150° oven.

Per serving: 675 calories, 22 g protein, 55 g carbohydrates, 42 g total fat, 328 mg cholesterol, 524 mg sodium

For breakfast, brunch, or supper, this rendition of Huevos Rancheros (recipe on facing page)
is sure to please. There's a spicy cooked sauce as well as Salsa Fresca
(page 40); black beans (page 69) are a typical accompaniment.

SIDE DISHES

VEGETABLES & SALADS

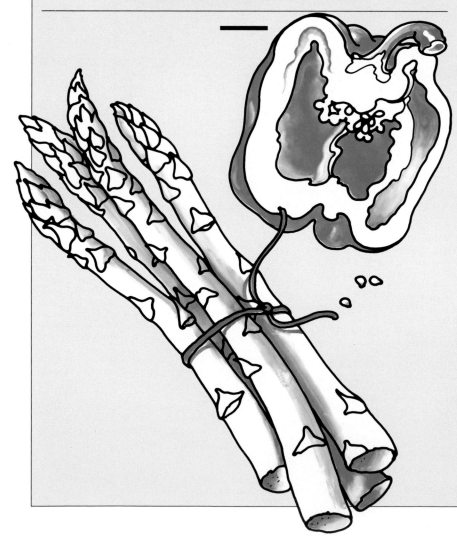

Beans, corn, and rice have traditionally been served with the rich chilis, stews, and barbecued meats of the Southwest; Black Beans simmered with salt pork and Baked Corn Pudding are typical choices. Fresh vegetables and salads, though, are relatively recent arrivals on the scene. Irrigation, provided by the federal dam system built in the 1930s, helped turn rangeland into farmland, bringing the region an abundance of fruits and vegetables.

Today's Southwestern cooks enjoy experimenting with fresh produce, often devising dishes with pleasing contrasts of flavor and texture— spicy green chiles filled with mild cheeses, for example, or tender black beans paired with crisp greens and juicy pineapple. Vegetables such as onions, tomatoes, peppers, and corn are often simply cooked on the grill along with a steak or other meat, but fruit and vegetable salads are just as popular; Orange & Avocado Salad and Asparagus with Tomatillos are two refreshing choices.

In addition to presenting vegetable dishes and salads, we've included a delicious innovation—homemade pastas made with puréed sweet bell peppers or chiles. One taste will convince you to feature these pastas in your menu planning.

BLACK BEANS

Pictured on front cover

Preparation time: 15 to 20 minutes
Cooking time: 2 to 2½ hours

The full, rich flavor of black beans, sometimes called turtle beans, belies their size. Serve them as a side dish with meats or poultry.

- ½ pound salt pork, diced
- 1 large onion, chopped
- 2 cloves garlic, minced or pressed
- 2½ cups (about 1 lb.) dried black beans, sorted, washed, and drained
- About 5 cups water
- 4 cups regular-strength beef broth
- Salt

In a 4- to 5-quart pan over medium heat, cook salt pork until fat begins to melt. Add onion and garlic and cook, stirring often, until onion is soft (about 10 minutes). Add beans, water, and broth. Bring to a boil over high heat; then reduce heat, cover, and simmer until beans are tender to bite (2 to 2½ hours). If beans are soupier than you like, uncover and boil over medium-high heat, stirring more frequently as mixture thickens. Season to taste with salt. Makes 6 to 8 servings.

Per serving: 443 calories, 17 g protein, 41 g carbohydrates, 24 g total fat, 24 mg cholesterol, 884 mg sodium

SWEET POTATOES WITH TEQUILA & LIME

Preparation time: 10 to 15 minutes
Cooking time: About 20 minutes

Keep this unusual sweet potato dish in mind when you're barbecuing poultry or pork. It can be made ahead, then reheated just before serving.

- ¾ cup (¼ lb. plus ¼ cup) butter or margarine
- 2 pounds sweet potatoes
- 2 tablespoons sugar
- 2 tablespoons tequila
- 1 tablespoon lime juice
- Salt and pepper
- Lime wedges

Place a 12- to 14-inch frying pan over medium heat; add butter and stir until melted. Set aside.

Peel sweet potatoes, then shred, using a food processor or coarse holes of a grater. Immediately mix with butter in pan, then sprinkle with sugar. Cook over medium heat until potatoes begin to caramelize and look slightly translucent (about 15 minutes); turn occasionally with a wide spatula.

Stir in tequila and lime juice. Cook, stirring, for 3 more minutes. Season to taste with salt and pepper. If made ahead, cover and refrigerate until next day; to serve, warm for about 15 minutes over medium-low heat, stirring occasionally.

Pour sweet potatoes into a bowl; garnish with lime. Makes 6 to 8 servings.

Per serving: 259 calories, 2 g protein, 23 g carbohydrates, 17 g total fat, 47 mg cholesterol, 187 mg sodium

BAKED CORN PUDDING

Preparation time: 20 to 25 minutes
Baking time: About 1 hour

Because you can make this sweet corn pudding a day ahead, it's a good choice for a buffet party. Try it with barbecued turkey or beef.

- 6 tablespoons butter or margarine
- 1 large onion, chopped
- 1 clove garlic, minced or pressed
- 1 *each* medium-size red and green bell pepper, seeded and chopped
- ⅓ cup all-purpose flour
- 1 teaspoon salt
- 1 tablespoon sugar
- ¼ teaspoon pepper
- 2 cans (about 1 lb. *each*) cream-style corn
- 6 eggs, lightly beaten
- 2 cups milk

Melt butter in a 5-quart pan over medium heat; add onion, garlic, and bell peppers. Cook, stirring often, until onion is soft (about 10 minutes). Stir in flour, salt, sugar, and pepper; cook, stirring, until bubbly. Remove from heat; add corn, eggs, and milk, stirring until mixture is well blended.

Pour corn mixture into a buttered shallow 3-quart baking dish. (At this point, you may cover and refrigerate until next day.)

Bake, uncovered, in a 350° oven until center appears set when dish is gently shaken (about 55 minutes; 65 minutes if refrigerated). Makes 10 servings.

Per serving: 233 calories, 8 g protein, 26 g carbohydrates, 12 g total fat, 190 mg cholesterol, 615 mg sodium

Lightly blistered, then split and stuffed, Grilled Chiles Rellenos with Shrimp
(recipe on facing page) are heated on the barbecue. Diners top servings with Tomatillo Salsa
(page 40) and sour cream, then enjoy chiles as a side dish or light entrée.

70

ZUCCHINI WITH CORN & PEPPERS

Preparation time: 10 to 15 minutes
Cooking time: About 5 minutes

You can prepare these vegetables ahead, but for bright color and crisp texture, quickly sauté them just before serving.

> 3 tablespoons butter or margarine
> 2½ pounds zucchini, cut into ¼-inch slices
> About 1½ cups fresh corn kernels, or 1 package (10 oz.) frozen whole-kernel corn, thawed
> 1 red bell pepper, seeded and chopped
> 1 medium-size onion, chopped
> 2 cloves garlic, minced or pressed
> Salt and pepper

Melt butter in a wide frying pan over high heat; add zucchini, corn, bell pepper, onion, and garlic. Cook, stirring often, until vegetables are tender-crisp to bite (about 5 minutes). Season to taste with salt and pepper. Makes 8 to 10 servings.

Per serving: 72 calories, 2 g protein, 9 g carbohydrates, 4 g total fat, 9 mg cholesterol, 43 mg sodium

ROASTED CHEESE-STUFFED CHILES

Preparation time: About 5 minutes
Baking time: 25 minutes

This quick-to-assemble accompaniment gives a mild, distinctive spark to almost any menu. Try it with grilled meats, poultry, or scrambled eggs.

> 4 large fresh mild red or green chiles such as Anaheim
> ½ cup *each* shredded Cheddar and mozzarella cheese

Leaving stems on, slit chiles lengthwise and discard seeds and ribs. Mix cheeses and fill chiles equally with cheese.

Place chiles, side by side and slit side up, in a 9-inch square baking pan. Bake, uncovered, in a 400° oven until chiles are soft and lightly tinged with brown (about 25 minutes). Makes 4 servings.

Per serving: 127 calories, 8 g protein, 8 g carbohydrates, 8 g total fat, 26 mg cholesterol, 146 mg sodium

GRILLED CHILES RELLENOS WITH SHRIMP

Pictured on facing page

Preparation time: About 30 minutes
Grilling time: 7 to 10 minutes

Distinctively simple describes these grilled chiles stuffed with cooked shrimp. They're good with Quesadillas (page 37), or scrambled eggs.

> Tomatillo Salsa (page 40)
> 8 to 12 large fresh mild green chiles such as Anaheim (6 to 6½ inches long) or fresh poblano chiles (3 to 5 inches long)
> 1 pound small cooked shrimp
> ¾ cup thinly sliced green onions (including tops)
> Sour cream

Prepare Tomatillo Salsa; cover and refrigerate.

Using a barbecue with a lid, place chiles on a lightly greased grill 4 to 6 inches above a solid bed of hot coals. Cook, uncovered, until chiles are blistered and slightly charred on 1 side (2 to 3 minutes). Remove from heat; peel any blistered skin that comes off easily. Slit each chile lengthwise down cooked side. Scrape out seeds but leave chiles whole.

Mix shrimp and onions; fill chiles equally. Place chiles, slit side up, on grill 4 to 6 inches above a solid bed of medium coals. Put lid on barbecue. Cook without turning until shrimp mixture is hot to touch (5 to 7 minutes). With a wide spatula, transfer chiles to plates. Serve with salsa and sour cream. Makes 4 entrée servings, 8 to 12 side dish servings.

Per serving: 221 calories, 32 g protein, 23 g carbohydrates, 2 g total fat, 170 mg cholesterol, 176 mg sodium

GRILLED CHILES RELLENOS WITH CORN

Prepare **Blender Salsa** (page 41); cover and refrigerate. Prepare chiles as for **Grilled Chiles Rellenos with Shrimp.** For the filling, melt 2 tablespoons **butter** or margarine in a wide frying pan over medium heat; add 1 large **onion,** chopped, and 1 medium-size **red bell pepper,** seeded and chopped. Cook, stirring often, until onion is soft (about 10 minutes).

Add 2 cups **corn kernels,** fresh or frozen (thawed if frozen), and cook, stirring, until corn is hot. Let cool, then stir in 1 cup (about 4 oz.) ½-inch cubes of **Cheddar cheese;** evenly spoon into chiles.

Cook as for **Grilled Chiles Rellenos with Shrimp,** increasing grilling time to 8 to 10 minutes. Serve with **Blender Salsa.** Makes 8 to 12 servings.

ROASTED ONIONS

Preparation time: 5 minutes
Baking time: 1 to 1¼ hours

Soft, mellow onions, enhanced with a sweet-sour glaze, go well with roast beef, turkey, pork chops, or sausages.

> ¾ **cup water**
> ½ **cup balsamic or red wine vinegar**
> 2 **teaspoons firmly packed brown sugar**
> ⅛ **teaspoon pepper**
> 4 **medium-size onions**
> **Salt**

Blend water, vinegar, sugar, and pepper. Pour into a 9- by 13-inch baking pan. Cut onions in half lengthwise through skins; place, cut side down, in vinegar mixture.

Bake, uncovered, in lower third of a 400° oven until onions give readily when gently squeezed and cut sides are glazed (1 to 1¼ hours). Arrange, cut side up, on a platter. Season to taste with salt. Makes 8 servings.

Per serving: 20 calories, .47 g protein, 5 g carbohydrates, .1 g total fat, 0 mg cholesterol, 1 mg sodium

BLACK BEAN SALAD WITH PINEAPPLE

Preparation time: About 2½ to 3 hours
Chilling time: 4 hours or until next day

Fresh pineapple and nippy mustard greens offer an intriguing background for mellow black beans colorfully dressed with a bell pepper vinaigrette.

> **Herb Bouquet (directions follow)**
> **Bell Pepper Vinaigrette (recipe follows)**
> 1¼ **cups (about ½ lb.) dried black beans, sorted, washed, and drained**
> 4 **cups regular-strength beef broth**
> 1 **orange, unpeeled, cut in half**
> 6 **large mustard green leaves**
> 6 **round slices fresh pineapple, halved**
> **Red, green, or yellow bell pepper slices**

Prepare Herb Bouquet and Bell Pepper Vinaigrette; set aside separately.

In a 3- to 4-quart pan, combine beans, broth, orange, and Herb Bouquet. Bring to a boil over high

heat; then reduce heat, cover, and simmer until beans are tender to bite (2 to 2½ hours). Drain liquid; discard orange and Herb Bouquet, and stir in Bell Pepper Vinaigrette. Cover and refrigerate for at least 4 hours or until next day.

Line 6 salad plates with mustard greens. Mound bean mixture on top and garnish with pineapple and bell pepper. Makes 6 servings.

HERB BOUQUET. In 3 layers of cheesecloth, tie 1 medium-size **onion**, quartered; 4 cloves **garlic**, halved; 1 tablespoon *each* **dry oregano leaves, dry thyme leaves,** and **dry basil;** and 2 **dry bay leaves.**

BELL PEPPER VINAIGRETTE. Combine ½ cup *each* **olive oil** and chopped **red, green, or yellow bell pepper;** 3 tablespoons *each* finely chopped **onion** and **balsamic or red wine vinegar;** 2 teaspoons **Dijon mustard;** and ½ teaspoon **ground cumin.**

Per serving: 389 calories, 13 g protein, 45 g carbohydrates, 20 g total fat, 0 mg cholesterol, 688 mg sodium

ORANGE & AVOCADO SALAD WITH CUMIN VINAIGRETTE

Preparation time: 20 to 25 minutes
Standing time for dressing: At least 1 hour

This salad offers a welcome, cooling contrast to fiery entrées. It's a good choice for a help-yourself chili buffet.

> **Cumin Vinaigrette (recipe follows)**
> 4 **medium-size oranges**
> 2 **large ripe avocados**
> 2 **green onions (including tops), thinly sliced**

Prepare Cumin Vinaigrette; set aside.

With a sharp knife cut peel and all white membrane from oranges. Cut crosswise into ¼-inch-thick slices. Pit and peel avocados; cut lengthwise into ½-inch-thick wedges. Arrange oranges and avocados on a platter; top with vinaigrette and sprinkle with onions. Serve, or let stand for up to 1 hour at room temperature. Makes 6 to 8 servings.

CUMIN VINAIGRETTE. Whisk together 5 tablespoons **salad oil;** 1 tablespoon **balsamic or red wine vinegar;** 1 tablespoon **orange juice;** 1 teaspoon **sugar;** ¼ teaspoon **ground cumin;** and 1 clove **garlic,** minced or pressed. Season to taste with **salt** and **pepper.** Cover and let stand for at least 1 hour to let flavors blend.

Per serving: 215 calories, 2 g protein, 14 g carbohydrates, 18 g total fat, 0 mg cholesterol, 7 mg sodium

Bell Pepper or Chile Pasta

Mellow to assertive, bell peppers and chiles can pack a flavor surprise into colorful homemade pasta. You begin by roasting fresh bell peppers or chiles (or toasting and soaking dried ones), then puréeing them; the purée is used for part of the liquid in an egg-tender dough.

Make the pasta by hand or use a food processor and pasta machine. Cook it within a couple of hours, or store it airtight in the refrigerator for up to 2 days.

Present the pasta simply, with butter and cheese. Or, for a quick, complementary dressing, offer a sauce of pine nuts sautéed in butter with slivered red bell peppers.

Red Bell Pepper Pasta

Put 2 pounds (about 4 large) **red bell peppers** in a 9-inch square baking pan. Bake, uncovered, in a 450° oven, turning occasionally, until skins are blackened all over (40 to 45 minutes). Let cool for 5 minutes; then put peppers in a bag, seal, and let cool completely. Discard skins, stems, and seeds. Purée peppers in a blender or food processor.

In a 2-quart pan, stir purée over medium heat, until reduced to ½ cup (10 minutes). Let cool.

Place 2 cups **all-purpose flour** in a bowl; make a well in center, pour in purée, and add 1 **egg.** Stir with a fork until well mixed; dough will be crumbly. Shape into a ball and knead on a lightly floured board until dough is smooth (about 10 minutes); add **all-purpose flour** as needed to prevent sticking, using as little as possible. (Or place flour, purée, and egg in a food processor and whirl until dough forms a ball—at least 30 seconds.) Divide dough into sixths; cover with plastic wrap and let rest for at least 10 minutes.

Roll 1 portion of dough at a time on a lightly floured board until as thin as possible (¹⁄₁₆ to ¹⁄₃₂ inch thick). Use as little flour as possible. (Or roll dough with a pasta machine, following manufacturer's directions.)

Lay rolled sheets in a single layer on wax paper on a flat surface. Let dry, uncovered, until dough no longer feels tacky when stroked (about 50 minutes). Turn dough over 2 or 3 times as it dries.

When dough is dry, cut it into ¼-inch (or narrower) strips, using a sharp knife or pasta machine. Pile pasta in loose coils and cook within 2 hours. If made ahead, lay cut strands out straight in single layers on wax paper. Cover with wax paper, roll up, and place in plastic bags. Seal airtight and refrigerate for up to 2 days.

To cook pasta, bring 3 quarts **water** to boiling in a 5- to 6-quart pan over high heat. Drop in pasta; stir well. Cover and remove from heat; let stand until pasta is tender to bite (1 to 2 minutes). Drain well and pour onto a warm platter.

To serve, add ¼ cup hot melted **butter** or margarine and ½ cup grated **Parmesan cheese;** lift with forks to mix, then sprinkle with chopped **parsley.** Or toss with **Pine Nut–Butter Sauce** (recipe follows). At the table, offer additional grated cheese, **salt,** and **pepper.** Makes about 1 pound pasta or 4 servings.

Pine Nut–Butter Sauce. Stem and seed 1 medium-size **red bell pepper;** cut into slivers. In a small frying pan, combine pepper and ½ cup (¼ lb.) **butter** or margarine. Cook, stirring, over medium heat until pepper is soft (about 5 minutes). Stir in ¼ cup **pine nuts;** cook until toasted.

Poblano Chile Pasta

Follow directions for **Red Bell Pepper Pasta,** but use 2 pounds (about 6 to 8 large) **fresh poblano chiles** instead of bell peppers.

Dried Red Chile Pasta

Follow directions for **Red Bell Pepper Pasta,** but substitute 2 ounces (about 6) **dried red New Mexico or California chiles** for bell peppers. Place chiles in a single layer in a 9- by 13-inch baking pan. Bake, uncovered, in a 300° oven just until chiles smell toasted (about 4 minutes). Discard stems and seeds. Pour 8 cups **boiling water** over chiles. Soak for 1 hour, then drain. Purée chiles and 2 **eggs.** Combine purée and 2 cups **all-purpose flour** to make dough. Continue as directed.

ASPARAGUS WITH TOMATILLOS

Pictured on facing page

Preparation time: 15 to 20 minutes

Stately asparagus spears signal the arrival of spring. Here they star in a refreshing salad simply dressed with tomato and tart tomatillos.

- 1 **pound asparagus**
- 3 **tablespoons olive oil**
- 4 **large tomatillos (about 1½-inch-diameter), husked, cored, and finely diced**
- 1 **small Roma-type tomato, cored and finely diced**
- ¼ **cup finely shredded Parmesan cheese**
  Lemon wedges
  Salt and pepper

Snap off and discard tough ends of asparagus; rinse spears well. In a deep, wide frying pan, bring about 1 inch water to a boil over high heat; add asparagus and cook, uncovered, until barely tender when pierced (3 to 5 minutes). Drain and immerse in ice water. When cool, drain again; then arrange equally on 4 salad plates (or arrange all asparagus on a platter).

In a bowl, mix oil, tomatillos, and tomato; evenly spoon over asparagus. Sprinkle with cheese. Garnish with lemon wedges. Season to taste with salt and pepper. Makes 4 servings.

Per serving: 152 calories, 5 g protein, 7 g carbohydrates, 12 g total fat, 4 mg cholesterol, 96 mg sodium

CILANTRO SLAW

Pictured on page 59

Preparation time: 15 to 20 minutes

Cilantro and a touch of lime juice give this crisp slaw its special sophistication. Offer it with grilled meat, chili, or enchiladas.

- 1 **small head green cabbage (about 1 lb.), finely shredded**
- 1 **small onion, minced**
- 2 **tablespoons minced fresh cilantro (coriander)**
- 1 **English cucumber (about 1 lb.)**
  Lime & Garlic Dressing (recipe follows)
  Salt and pepper

Mix cabbage, onion, and cilantro. Peel and seed cucumber; cut into 3-inch-long sticks. (At this point, you may cover and refrigerate cabbage mixture and cucumber separately for up to 1 day.)

Prepare Lime & Garlic Dressing. Stir dressing into cabbage mixture; serve in a bowl or on a platter. Garnish with cucumber; season to taste with salt and pepper. Makes 6 to 8 servings.

LIME & GARLIC DRESSING. Whisk together ½ cup **salad oil**, ⅓ cup **lime juice**, and 2 cloves **garlic**, minced or pressed. If made ahead, cover and refrigerate for up to 2 days; stir to reblend before using.

Per serving: 146 calories, 1 g protein, 6 g carbohydrates, 14 g total fat, 0 mg cholesterol, 15 mg sodium

MARINATED BELL PEPPER STRIPS

Preparation time: 10 to 15 minutes
Chilling time: 1 week to 3 months

For a splash of color and flavor, serve these bell pepper strips on meat or cheese sandwiches; or dice them and add to salads, vegetables, or rice.

- 6 **large red or green bell peppers**
- 3 **large cloves garlic, thinly sliced**
- 1 **cup *each* salad oil, white wine vinegar, and water**
- 2 **teaspoons sugar**
- 4 **teaspoons seasoned salt**
- ½ **teaspoon pepper**
- 2 **medium-size onions, thinly sliced and separated into rings**

Cut bell peppers in half; remove stems, seeds, and membranes. Then cut each pepper half lengthwise into ¾-inch-wide strips.

In a 5- to 6-quart pan, combine garlic, oil, vinegar, water, sugar, salt, and pepper. Bring to a boil over high heat; add bell pepper strips and boil gently, stirring, for 3 minutes. Remove from heat, stir in onions, and spoon into a 3- to 4-quart glass or plastic container with a tight-fitting lid. Let cool, uncovered, then affix lid and refrigerate for at least 1 week before serving; stir several times. Refrigerated, strips will keep for up to 3 months. Makes 10 cups.

Per cup: 241 calories, 1 g protein, 11 g carbohydrates, 22 g total fat, 0 mg cholesterol, 494 mg sodium

Platter of Asparagus with Tomatillos (recipe on facing page) is ready for the
buffet table. Finely shredded Parmesan cheese tops the chunky
tomatillo-tomato mixture; a squeeze of lemon adds a refreshing accent.

FRESH BREADS

INCLUDING TORTILLAS

The truly indigenous breads of the Southwest are those handed down through generations of native Indians: Apache, Hopi, Navajo, Papago, Rio Grande Pueblo, Zuni, and others. Three of the most familiar—Paper Bread cooked over hot rocks, Ash Bread cooked in the coals of fires, and Navajo Fry Bread—are still enjoyed today. Modern directions for making these specialties are on page 81.

Sopaipillas, the pillowlike breads of New Mexico, are a descendant of Navajo Fry Bread. To serve these crisp puffs, split them in half and spread with butter and honey.

Breads with a Spanish-Mexican heritage are also very popular in the Southwest. Tortillas made of both wheat and corn flours have become a mainstay. Cornbreads, especially those made from earthy-flavored blue corn, are another favorite.

If you don't live in the Southwest but want to try the blue corn tortilla, muffin, or waffle recipes given here, turn to page 10 for information on where to buy blue cornmeal.

Two sweet bread recipes included in this chapter are buns flavored with anise, a popular spice for Southwestern holiday treats, and sticky buns topped with Texas-grown pecans.

HOMEMADE FLOUR OR FLOUR-MASA TORTILLAS

―――

Preparation time: About 30 minutes
Cooking time: 10 to 25 minutes, depending on number of tortillas made

―――

Tortillas are widely sold in the Southwest and many other parts of the country, but they are also easy to make. This recipe gives directions for making both plain flour tortillas and corn-flavored flour-masa tortillas in four sizes.

Serve tortillas warm with butter or in specialties such as burritos or Arizona Cheese Crisps (page 18).

―――

    2   to 2¼ cups all-purpose flour; or 1¼ to
        1½ cups all-purpose flour and ⅔ cup
        dehydrated masa flour (corn tortilla
        flour)
    ¼   cup lard or solid vegetable shortening
    1   teaspoon salt
    ½   cup lukewarm water
        Butter or margarine

―――

In a food processor, combine 2 cups all-purpose flour (or 1¼ cups all-purpose flour and the masa flour), lard, and salt. Whirl until fine, even crumbs form. Add water, ¼ cup at a time, and whirl until dough holds together. Or rub flour, lard, and salt together with your fingers until mixture forms fine crumbs; stir in water with a fork.

Pat dough into a ball and knead until smooth (about 1 minute). Divide dough into sixths, quarters, thirds, or halves; to prevent drying, keep dough covered with plastic wrap.

On a lightly floured board, roll dough sixths into 9-inch rounds, dough quarters into 12-inch rounds, dough thirds into 15-inch rounds, or dough halves into 18-inch rounds. Turn frequently and add flour as needed to prevent sticking.

On an ungreased griddle, 12- by 17-inch baking sheet, or 14-inch pizza pan, cook each tortilla over medium heat until it looks dry and is speckled with brown on each side. (If tortilla overlaps pan, use tongs or your fingers to slide it around and to hold it away from burner.) Stack tortillas as you cook them. Serve warm with butter. If made ahead, let cool, wrap airtight, and refrigerate for up to 2 days. To reheat tortillas, stack and wrap in foil, then place in a 350° oven for about 15 minutes. Makes six 9-inch tortillas, four 12-inch tortillas, three 15-inch tortillas, or two 18-inch tortillas.

Per 9" tortilla: 248 calories, 5 g protein, 36 g carbohydrates, 9 g total fat, 8 mg cholesterol, 368 mg sodium

SANTA FE FLOUR TORTILLAS

―――

Preparation time: About 30 minutes
Cooking time: 20 to 30 minutes

―――

Santa Fe–style flour tortillas are unlike any others; they're both lighter and thicker. They are especially good served warm with butter; you can also use them as burrito wrappers.

―――

        About 5 cups all-purpose flour
    4   teaspoons baking powder
    1   teaspoon salt
        About ½ cup solidified bacon drippings
        or solid vegetable shortening
    2   cups buttermilk

―――

In a large bowl, combine 5 cups of the flour with baking powder and salt. With a pastry blender or 2 knives, cut ½ cup of the bacon drippings into dry ingredients until fine, even crumbs form. Slowly add buttermilk, stirring with a fork to make a soft, non-sticky dough. Knead in bowl for 3 to 5 minutes.

Divide dough into 10 pieces. Shape each into a smooth ball; to prevent drying, keep covered with plastic wrap. On a lightly floured board, flatten each ball of dough to make a 3- to 4-inch round. Roll each into a 7-inch circle, ⅜ inch thick.

To cook, preheat a griddle or electric frying pan to 375°. Coat surface well with bacon drippings. Turn tortillas onto griddle, 1 at a time. Cook each tortilla until bubbly and browned, turning once (2 to 3 minutes per side).

As tortillas come off griddle, put them in a 250° oven (directly on rack) for 5 minutes. Remove tortillas from rack, stack them, and wrap in foil. Return to warm oven until serving or for up to 1 hour. Makes 10 tortillas.

Per tortilla: 322 calories, 8 g protein, 50 g carbohydrates, 9 g total fat, 9 mg cholesterol, 495 mg sodium

―――

CRISP-FRIED TORTILLA PIECES

―――

Cut 6- to 7-inch-diameter **corn tortillas** into pie-shaped wedges (fourths, sixths, or eighths). In a wide frying pan, heat about 1 inch **salad oil** over medium-high heat to 350°F on a deep-frying thermometer. Add tortilla pieces, a few at a time; cook, turning occasionally, until crisp and lightly browned (30 to 60 seconds). Drain on paper towels; sprinkle lightly with **salt,** if desired. Store airtight.

New Mexico's ancient staple, flour ground from blue corn, produces this bowlful of
distinctive treats—Blue Corn Tortillas and Blue Corn Muffins
(recipes on facing page) and Blue Corn Waffles (recipe on page 80).

BLUE CORN TORTILLAS

Pictured on facing page

Preparation time: About 30 minutes
Cooking time: About 20 minutes

Flour ground from the kernels of blue corn produces these curiously colored tortillas. They have a more primitive flavor and a firmer, less flexible texture than regular corn tortillas.

Serve blue tortillas warm with butter or with any taco filling, or use them in Flat Blue Enchiladas (page 42).

2 **cups blue cornmeal for tortillas**
   (*harina para tortillas*)
¼ **teaspoon salt**
1 **cup warm water**

Cut 24 pieces of wax paper, each about 6 inches square. Set aside.

In a bowl, mix cornmeal, salt, and water until cornmeal is moistened. Cover bowl with plastic wrap and let dough stand for at least 2 minutes; keep covered at all times to prevent drying.

Divide dough into 12 equal pieces and quickly roll each piece into a ball; flatten slightly and return to covered bowl. Shape and cook tortillas 1 at a time.

To shape with a tortilla press, cover bottom half of press with a square of wax paper and set a dough round on paper. Lay another piece of wax paper on dough and close press tightly. Open press; peel off top paper.

To shape with a rolling pin, place a piece of dough between 2 pieces of wax paper; flatten slightly with your hand. Lightly run a rolling pin over dough several times. Flip dough and paper over and continue to roll out until a ragged 6-inch circle is formed. Carefully peel off top paper.

To make a perfectly shaped tortilla, cut dough into a 5- to 6-inch circle with the end of a 2-pound coffee can. Let tortilla stand, uncovered, for 1 to 2 minutes to dry slightly.

To cook, place a cast-iron or other heavy 10- to 12-inch frying pan or griddle over medium-high heat. When pan is hot, lift tortilla, supporting with paper, and turn over into pan. At once, peel off paper. Cook tortilla until surface looks dry and bottom side is flecked with brown (about 30 seconds). With a wide spatula, flip tortilla over and cook for 1 more minute; put on plate and cover with foil.

While 1 tortilla is cooking, shape another; cook it as you shape the next. Stack tortillas as baked and keep covered.

Tortillas are best as a bread if eaten warm. For other uses, store cooled tortillas in a plastic bag and refrigerate for up to 5 days (freeze for longer storage). Makes 12 tortillas.

Per tortilla: 84 calories, 2 g protein, 18 g carbohydrates, .27 g total fat, 0 mg cholesterol, 45 mg sodium

BLUE CORN MUFFINS

Pictured on facing page

Preparation time: 10 to 15 minutes
Baking time: About 20 minutes

Muffins made with blue cornmeal are sure to attract attention at a company brunch or dinner. Though similar to yellow cornmeal muffins, they have a moister texture and an earthy flavor.

1 **cup all-purpose flour**
1 **cup blue cornmeal for tortillas**
   (*harina para tortillas*) **or for** *atole*
   (*harina para atole*)
2 **tablespoons sugar**
1 **tablespoon baking powder**
½ **teaspoon salt**
2 **eggs**
1 **cup milk**
¼ **cup butter or margarine, melted**
   Butter or margarine
   Honey

In a large bowl, combine flour, cornmeal, sugar, baking powder, and salt. In another bowl, beat eggs, milk, and melted butter until blended. Pour liquids into dry mixture, stirring just to moisten. Spoon batter into 12 paper cup–lined or greased muffin cups (2½-inch size). Bake in a 400° oven until muffins are browned and a wooden pick inserted in center comes out clean (18 to 20 minutes). Serve hot with butter and honey.

If made ahead, let cool on racks and store airtight at room temperature until next day (freeze for longer storage). To reheat, thaw if frozen. Arrange muffins on a baking sheet; place in a 350° oven until warm (about 10 minutes). Makes 12 muffins.

Per muffin: 148 calories, 4 g protein, 20 g carbohydrates, 6 g total fat, 59 mg cholesterol, 258 mg sodium

Blue Corn Waffles

Pictured on page 78

Preparation time: About 15 minutes
Cooking time: 4 to 5 minutes per waffle; about 20 minutes total

Brush your waffle iron with melted butter before baking these crisp, light waffles; serve them with butter and maple syrup.

- 1½ cups blue cornmeal for tortillas (*harina para tortillas*)
- ¾ cup all-purpose flour
- 1 tablespoon sugar
- 2 teaspoons baking powder
- ½ teaspoon *each* baking soda and salt
- 1½ cups buttermilk
- 2 eggs, separated
- 6 tablespoons butter or margarine, melted

In a large bowl, mix cornmeal, flour, sugar, baking powder, baking soda, and salt.

In another bowl, mix buttermilk with egg yolks and ¼ cup melted butter. Pour liquids into dry mixture, stirring to moisten well. In another bowl, beat egg whites until stiff peaks form; fold into batter.

To bake, preheat a waffle iron to medium-high heat (375°) or as manufacturer directs. Brush grids with melted butter; half-fill waffle iron with batter, spreading slightly. Close iron and bake until waffle is golden brown (about 5 minutes). Repeat with remaining batter. Serve hot. Makes four 9-inch-square waffles.

Per 9" waffle: 516 calories, 13 g protein, 67 g carbohydrates, 22 g total fat, 187 mg cholesterol, 897 mg sodium

Mexicana Cornbread

Preparation time: About 20 minutes
Baking time: About 35 minutes

Laden with bits of cheese, olive, tomato, and avocado, this cornbread has a moist texture as well as a colorful appearance. Serve it alongside scrambled eggs.

- 1 cup *each* yellow cornmeal and all-purpose flour
- 1 tablespoon baking powder
- ½ teaspoon *each* salt and ground cumin
- ¼ teaspoon paprika
- 1 egg
- 1 cup milk
- ¼ cup salad oil
- 1 cup diced avocado
- ¼ cup *each* chopped onion and peeled, seeded, chopped tomato
- 2 tablespoons finely chopped fresh or canned serrano chiles (optional)
- ½ cup shredded sharp Cheddar cheese
- 3 tablespoons sliced ripe olives

In a large bowl, mix cornmeal, flour, baking powder, salt, cumin, and paprika. Set aside. In another bowl, beat egg lightly, then stir in milk, oil, avocado, onion, tomato, chiles (if used), and cheese. Stir milk mixture into dry ingredients just until evenly moistened.

Pour batter into a greased 8-inch square baking pan. Sprinkle olives on top. Bake in a 400° oven until a wooden pick inserted in center comes out clean (35 minutes). Let cool slightly; cut into squares. Makes 9 servings.

Per serving: 247 calories, 6 g protein, 26 g carbohydrates, 13 g total fat, 41 mg cholesterol, 347 mg sodium

Jalapeño Spoonbread

Preparation time: About 20 minutes
Baking time: About 40 to 50 minutes

The fire of jalapeño chiles combines with cumin, corn, and Cheddar cheese to give this spoonable, puddinglike bread an authoritative flavor.

- 2 eggs
- 2 cans (about 1 lb. *each*) cream-style corn
- 1 small onion, finely chopped
- 1 can (2¼ oz.) sliced ripe olives, drained
- ⅓ cup salad oil
- 4 to 7 jalapeño chiles, stemmed, seeded, and finely chopped
- 1 teaspoon *each* garlic salt and baking powder
- ½ teaspoon ground cumin
- ¾ cup yellow cornmeal
- 2 cups (8 oz.) shredded Cheddar cheese

In a large bowl, beat eggs; add corn, onion, olives, oil, and chiles. Set aside. In another bowl, combine garlic salt, baking powder, cumin, and cornmeal. Add to egg mixture with 1 cup of the cheese; stir to blend.

Pour batter into a well-greased 9-inch cast-iron frying pan or 9-inch square baking pan; scatter remaining 1 cup cheese over top.

Bake in a 350° oven until golden brown (about 40 to 50 minutes). Spoon out of pan. Makes 6 servings.

Per serving: 499 calories, 17 g protein, 48 g carbohydrates, 29 g total fat, 131 mg cholesterol, 1,142 mg sodium

INDIAN BREADS

The breads of the Southwest Indians are an important part of the area's heritage. Hopi-style Paper Bread—flaky sheets of cornmeal traditionally cooked on a hot "piki" stone—has a toasted popcorn flavor. For our griddle version, you can use blue or yellow cornmeal.

Ash Bread, made of wheat flour, is a big biscuit traditionally baked in a heavy pot among hot coals. We give directions for preparing it in your oven.

Golden, puffy Fry Bread ("Papago popover") can be served as a sweet bread with powdered sugar or like a tortilla, wrapped around foods.

ASH BREAD

In a large bowl, stir together 2 cups **all-purpose flour,** 1 tablespoon **baking powder,** and ½ teaspoon **salt.** Add 6 tablespoons **lard** or solid vegetable shortening; with your fingers, rub mixture until evenly combined. Add ¾ cup **milk** and stir with a fork until dough clings together. Turn out onto a floured board and knead 5 or 6 times.

Pat dough evenly into a greased 8- or 9-inch ovenproof frying pan or pie pan. Bake, uncovered, in a 450° oven until golden brown (about 20 minutes).

To serve, cut bread into wedges; serve with **butter** or margarine. Makes 6 to 8 servings.

FRY BREAD

In a large bowl, stir together 2 cups **all-purpose flour,** ½ cup **instant nonfat dry milk,** 1 tablespoon **baking powder,** and ½ teaspoon **salt.** Add 2 tablespoons **lard** or solid vegetable shortening. With your fingers, rub mixture until evenly combined. Add ¾ cup **water** and stir with a fork until dough clings together.

Turn dough out onto a floured board and knead until smooth and satiny (about 3 minutes). Divide dough into 6 equal portions; shape each into a ball, then flatten to form a 6- to 7-inch round.

In a 3- to 4-quart pan, heat 1½ inches **salad oil** to 375°F on a deep-frying thermometer. Cook rounds of dough, 1 at a time, in oil until puffy and golden brown (about 2 minutes); turn once or twice. Drain on paper towels.

Serve breads hot; you can keep them warm in a 300° oven until all are cooked. Or wrap airtight and refrigerate until next day. To reheat, arrange in a single layer on a baking sheet and place in a 375° oven until hot (5 to 8 minutes).

Top bread with **powdered sugar** or honey and eat out of hand. Makes 6 servings.

PAPER BREAD

In a 3- to 4-quart pan, combine ¼ cup **yellow cornmeal** or blue cornmeal for tortillas *(harina para tortillas)* and ¾ teaspoon **salt.** Smoothly blend in 7 cups **water.** Bring to a boil over high heat, stirring with a long spoon (mixture spatters). Reduce heat to low and simmer, uncovered, for 15 minutes; stir occasionally.

Mix 1 cup **water** with ¼ cup **cornstarch.** Blend into cornmeal mixture; return to boiling and cook for 1 minute, stirring. Remove from heat.

Heat an electric griddle to 350° (or place a regular griddle over medium heat; it's ready when a drop of water dances). To prevent spatters, you can construct a wall of foil on 3 sides of griddle.

Coat griddle with **lard** or solid vegetable shortening. Pour ⅓ to ½ cup of corn gruel onto griddle (watch out for hot spatters); with a long, flexible spatula, gently guide liquid to form a rectangle, about 8 by 10 inches. Cook until bread is dry and pulls from griddle (about 5 minutes). With dry spatula and fingers, gently lift bread from griddle.

Grease griddle and cook another sheet of paper bread; when half dry, lay cooked sheet of paper bread directly on top (if cooked bread breaks, use pieces). Continue to cook until bread pulls from griddle (about 15 more minutes) to make a double-thick piece of bread. Loosely fold hot sheets (bread will break).

Repeat procedure to make each piece of bread. Serve at room temperature; or let cool, then store airtight at room temperature for up to 1 week. Makes 6 to 8 pieces.

SOPAIPILLAS

―

Pictured on facing page

Preparation time: About 40 minutes, plus 1 hour to rise
Cooking time: 20 to 30 minutes

These light and airy pillows of fried bread are served at various courses of a Southwestern meal. They can be split and filled with cold cuts to make a sandwich, used as soft tacos with meat fillings, made into bread pudding, or simply served warm with butter and honey.

  1 **package active dry yeast**
  ¼ **cup warm water (about 110°F)**
1½ **cups milk**
  3 **tablespoons lard or solid vegetable shortening**
  1 **teaspoon salt**
  2 **tablespoons sugar**
  1 **cup whole wheat flour**
     About 4 cups all-purpose flour
     Salad oil

In a large bowl, dissolve yeast in water and set aside.

In a 1½- to 2-quart pan, combine milk, lard, salt, and sugar; heat to 110°F and add to dissolved yeast. With a dough hook or a heavy spoon, beat in whole wheat flour and 3 cups of the all-purpose flour until dough is stretchy.

Knead dough on a lightly floured board, adding as little remaining flour as necessary to prevent sticking, until smooth and satiny. Place dough in a greased bowl; turn to grease top. Cover with plastic wrap; let rise for 1 hour at room temperature.

Punch dough down and knead briefly to expel air. On a lightly floured board, roll ¼ of the dough at a time into a rectangle about ⅛ inch thick. Cut into 6 equal pieces; place on lightly floured pans and cover with plastic wrap. (At this point, you may refrigerate sopaipillas until ready to fry or until next day.)

In a deep 3- to 4-quart pan, heat 2 inches oil to 350°F on a deep-frying thermometer. Fry 2 or 3 sopaipillas at a time. When bread puffs, gently push portion where bubble is developing into hot oil to help sopaipilla puff evenly. Cook until pale gold, turning several times (1 to 2 minutes *total*). Drain on paper towels.

Serve sopaipillas warm. If made ahead, let cool, then cover and refrigerate for up to 2 days (freeze for longer storage). To reheat, thaw if frozen. Arrange on baking sheets and bake, uncovered, in a 300° oven,

turning once, until warm (5 to 8 minutes). Do not overheat or sopaipillas will harden. Makes 2 dozen sopaipillas.

Per sopaipilla: 141 calories, 3 g protein, 21 g carbohydrates, 5 g total fat, 4 mg cholesterol, 100 mg sodium

SHEEPHERDER'S BREAD

―

Preparation time: About 40 minutes, plus 2½ hours to rise
Baking time: About 50 minutes

Through the years, the staff of life for Basque sheepherders in Southwest rangelands has been a big, puffy loaf of white bread. They bake their bread in Dutch ovens buried in pits—but for more reliable results, you can bake it in a conventional oven.

  3 **cups very hot tap water**
  ½ **cup (¼ lb.) butter or margarine**
  ⅓ **cup sugar**
  2 **teaspoons salt**
  2 **packages active dry yeast**
     About 9½ cups all-purpose flour
     Salad oil

In a large bowl, combine water, butter, sugar, and salt. Stir until butter is melted; let cool to about 110°F. Stir in yeast and set in a warm place until bubbly (about 5 minutes).

With a heavy spoon, beat in about 5 cups of the flour to make a thick batter. Stir in about 3½ cups more flour or enough to make a stiff dough.

Knead dough on a lightly floured board, adding as little remaining flour as necessary to prevent sticking, until smooth and satiny (10 to 20 minutes). Place dough in a greased bowl; turn to grease top. Cover with plastic wrap; let rise in a warm place until doubled (about 1½ hours).

Punch dough down and knead briefly to expel air. Shape into a smooth ball. Cover the inside bottom of a 5-quart cast-iron or cast-aluminum Dutch oven with a circle of foil. Grease foil and underside of lid with oil.

Place dough in Dutch oven and cover with lid. Let rise in a warm place until dough pushes up lid by ½ inch (about 1 hour); watch closely.

Bake, covered, in a 375° oven for 12 minutes. Uncover and continue to bake until loaf is golden brown (30 to 35 more minutes). Remove from oven and turn out onto a rack (you'll need a helper). Peel off foil, turn loaf upright, and let cool. Makes 1 very large loaf, 24 to 26 servings.

Per serving: 213 calories, 5 g protein, 37 g carbohydrates, 5 g total fat, 10 mg cholesterol, 207 mg sodium

Puffy, golden Sopaipillas (recipe on facing page), dusted with powdered sugar, are served with
comb honey and butter at this Southwestern brunch.
Also on the menu are salsa-topped scrambled eggs and fresh strawberries.

BEVERAGES

Are you looking for a special breakfast or dessert drink, or a cool punch to serve at an open house or as an apéritif? On this page, you'll find several favorite beverages from the Southwest, suitable for a variety of menus. There are five punches: two Sangritas, based on juice alone, and three appealing wine punches. For a special treat, try our New Mexican Hot Chocolate—rich enough for dessert.

TOMATO-ORANGE SANGRITA

In a large pitcher, combine 1 cup **tomato juice**, 2 cups **orange juice**, ½ cup **lemon or lime juice**, and ¼ teaspoon **liquid hot pepper seasoning.** Pour into ice-filled tumblers. Add **green onions** (with tops) for stirrers. Makes 4 servings.

TOMATO-CRANBERRY SANGRITA

In a large pitcher, combine 1½ cups *each* **tomato juice** and **cranberry juice cocktail,** ½ cup **lime juice,** and ¼ teaspoon **liquid hot pepper seasoning.** Pour into ice-filled tumblers. Add **green onions** (with tops) for stirrers. Makes 4 servings.

FRUITED SANGRIA PUNCH

Pictured on front cover

Up to a day ahead, stir together ¼ cup *each* **sugar** and **orange-flavored liqueur.** Add 1 medium-size **orange,** thinly sliced and seeded. Cover and refrigerate; stir occasionally. In a punch bowl, combine sugar mixture with 1 bottle (1.5 liters) cold **rosé,** 1 bottle (750 ml.) cold **burgundy,** 1 cup **orange juice,** and ⅓ cup **sugar.** Before serving, add 1 unpeeled **red-skinned apple** (thinly sliced) and **ice cubes.** Makes 3 quarts.

SPICY RED WINE PUNCH

In a 6-quart pan, combine 3½ quarts **water,** 3 cups **sugar,** and 6 **cinnamon sticks** (*each* 3 inches long), broken in half. Bring to boiling over high heat; then boil rapidly until reduced to 3 quarts (about 15 minutes). Remove cinnamon sticks.

Meanwhile, peel, core, and thinly slice 3 medium-size **Golden Delicious apples.** Mix with 2 tablespoons **lemon juice;** add to syrup, then add 1 cup *each* **raisins** and whole **pitted prunes** and 1 bottle (1.5 liters) **dry red wine.** (At this point, you may cover and refrigerate until next day.)

To serve, heat wine mixture to steaming; stir in ¾ cup **rum.** Transfer to a heatproof serving bowl; ladle punch and fruit into cups. Makes 4½ quarts.

MARGARITA WINE PUNCH

In a punch bowl, stir together 3 cans (6 oz. *each*) thawed **frozen limeade concentrate,** 1 can (12 oz.) thawed **frozen lemonade concentrate,** and 1 bottle (1.5 liters) plus 1 bottle (750 ml.) cold **dry white wine.** Shortly before serving, add **ice cubes.** Makes 3 quarts.

NEW MEXICAN HOT CHOCOLATE

Pictured on page 86

In a 2-quart pan, combine 4 cups **milk** and 3 **cinnamon sticks** (*each* 3 inches long); warm over low heat, stirring occasionally. Meanwhile, combine 6 ounces **bittersweet or semisweet chocolate** (broken into pieces), ⅓ cup **slivered almonds,** and 2 tablespoons **sugar** in a blender; whirl until a coarse powder forms. Turn heat to high and stir milk until just at the boiling point. Lift out cinnamon sticks and set aside. Pour half the milk into blender; cover (hold on lid with a thick towel) and whirl. Add remaining milk and whirl, covered, until blended. Split cinnamon sticks lengthwise into halves; put a section into each mug and fill with chocolate. Makes 6 servings.

CHORIZO BREAD

Preparation time: 15 to 20 minutes
Baking time: About 55 minutes

To purchase the fully cooked dry chorizo sausage that flavors this moist and hearty bread, you may need to visit a Mexican market. If chorizo is unavailable, pepperoni makes a satisfactory substitute.

About 5½ ounces dry chorizo or pepperoni sausage
3 cups all-purpose flour
3 tablespoons grated Parmesan cheese
2 tablespoons firmly packed brown sugar
4½ teaspoons baking powder
1 teaspoon fennel or caraway seeds
½ teaspoon salt
¼ teaspoon baking soda
1 small package (3 oz.) plus 1 large package (8 oz.) cream cheese, at room temperature
1 cup milk
2 eggs
¼ cup butter or margarine, melted

If necessary, remove sausage casing. Coarsely chop sausage; you should have 1 cup. Set aside. In a bowl, combine flour, Parmesan cheese, sugar, baking powder, fennel seeds, salt, and baking soda.

In another bowl, beat cream cheese until smooth; then stir in milk. Add eggs, 1 at a time, beating well. Stir in butter and chorizo. Add to flour mixture, stirring just to moisten. Spoon batter into a greased 5- by 9-inch loaf pan.

Bake in a 375° oven until bread browns and begins to pull away from pan sides (about 55 minutes). Let cool in pan on a rack for 5 minutes, then turn out. Cut bread into thick slices and serve warm.

If made ahead, let cool, wrap airtight, and store at room temperature for up to 1 day (freeze for longer storage; thaw wrapped). Reheat, uncovered, in a 350° oven until warm throughout (about 15 minutes). Makes 1 loaf, 10 to 12 servings.

Per serving: 344 calories, 10 g protein, 28 g carbohydrates, 21 g total fat, 99 mg cholesterol, 695 mg sodium

GREEN CHILE BREAD

Preparation time: 40 to 45 minutes, plus 2½ hours to rise
Baking time: About 40 minutes

Pair slices of this subtly green-hued loaf with cheese or smoked meats to make sandwiches; or toast the sliced bread and serve it at brunch or supper topped with poached eggs.

1 can (7 oz.) diced green chiles
⅛ to ¼ teaspoon ground red pepper (cayenne), optional
1 package active dry yeast
¼ cup warm water (about 110°F)
½ cup milk
2 tablespoons butter or margarine
1 teaspoon salt
1 tablespoon sugar
4 to 4½ cups all-purpose flour

In a blender or food processor, whirl chiles until smoothly puréed; you should have ¾ cup. Taste purée; add red pepper if you want a hotter flavor.

In a large bowl, sprinkle yeast over water; let stand until softened (about 5 minutes). Meanwhile, in a 2- to 4-cup pan, heat milk and butter to 110°F (butter need not melt completely). Add to yeast along with salt, sugar, chile purée, and 1½ cups of the flour, stirring to moisten thoroughly.

Stir in 1½ cups more flour until moistened, then beat vigorously with a heavy spoon until dough is stretchy (about 10 minutes). Scrape out onto a board coated with 1 cup more flour and knead until smooth and satiny (about 8 minutes); add as little remaining flour as necessary to prevent sticking. Place dough in a greased bowl; turn to grease top.

Cover dough with plastic wrap and let rise in a warm place until doubled (about 1½ hours).

Punch dough down and knead briefly to expel air. Shape into a smooth loaf and place in a greased 5- by 9-inch loaf pan. Cover with plastic wrap and let rise in a warm place until dough has risen 1½ inches above pan rim (about 1 hour). Remove plastic wrap.

Bake in a 375° oven until golden brown (about 40 minutes). Turn out onto a rack to cool. Makes 1 loaf, 12 to 14 servings.

Per serving: 174 calories, 5 g protein, 33 g carbohydrates, 2 g total fat, 6 mg cholesterol, 266 mg sodium

Spicy New Mexican Hot Chocolate (recipe on page 84) is the perfect partner
for round, shiny New Mexico Anise Buns (recipe on facing page). For a traditional presentation,
beat the chocolate to a froth with a carved wooden *molinillo*.

New Mexico Anise Buns

Pictured on facing page

*Preparation time: About 20 minutes, plus
2 to 2½ hours to rise
Baking time: 15 minutes*

The delicate licorice flavor of anise seeds permeates these tender sweet rolls from New Mexico. You mix two teaspoons of seeds into the dough, then sprinkle more seeds atop the buns before baking.

Serve these buns warm from the oven; they're good plain, but you might also spread them with sweet butter and apple butter or your favorite jam.

- ¾ **cup milk**
- 2 **tablespoons butter or margarine**
- ⅓ **cup sugar**
  - **About 1 tablespoon anise seeds**
- ½ **teaspoon salt**
- 1 **package active dry yeast**
- ¼ **cup warm water (about 110°F)**
- 2 **eggs**
- 3½ **to 4 cups all-purpose flour**

In a 1- to 2-quart pan, combine milk, butter, sugar, 2 teaspoons of the anise seeds, and salt. Heat, stirring, until temperature reaches 110°F (butter need not melt completely).

Meanwhile, in a large bowl, dissolve yeast in warm water. Stir milk mixture and 1 of the eggs into yeast. Then gradually beat in 3 to 3½ cups flour to make a soft dough. Knead dough on a floured board, adding as little remaining flour as necessary to prevent sticking, until smooth and satiny (about 10 minutes). Place dough in a greased bowl; turn to grease top. Cover with plastic wrap; let rise in a warm place until doubled (1 to 1½ hours).

Punch dough down and knead briefly to expel air. Divide dough into 24 equal pieces. Shape pieces into smooth balls and place about 2 inches apart on lightly greased baking sheets. Beat remaining egg and brush it over buns, being careful not to let egg drip down sides of buns onto baking sheets. Then sprinkle buns with remaining anise seeds. Cover lightly and let rise in a warm place until almost doubled (about 45 minutes).

Bake, uncovered, in a 400° oven until richly browned (about 15 minutes). Makes 24 buns.

Per bun: 108 calories, 3 g protein, 19 g carbohydrates, 2 g total fat, 26 mg cholesterol, 65 mg sodium

Sticky Pecan Rolls

*Preparation time: 30 to 40 minutes, plus 1½ hours to rise
Baking time: 20 to 25 minutes*

Texas-grown pecans are featured in the buttery caramel-nut topping on these rolls. Since the rolls need to rise only once, they're a bit quicker to make than many yeast breads.

- ¼ **teaspoon baking soda**
- ¼ **cup granulated sugar**
- ½ **teaspoon salt**
- 1 **package active dry yeast**
  - **About 2½ cups all-purpose flour**
- 1 **cup buttermilk**
- 3 **tablespoons salad oil**
- 2 **tablespoons water**
- ⅓ **cup butter or margarine, melted**
- ½ **cup firmly packed brown sugar**
- 1 **cup chopped pecans**
- 1 **teaspoon ground cinnamon**

In large bowl of an electric mixer, combine baking soda, granulated sugar, salt, yeast, and 1 cup of the flour. Set aside.

Heat buttermilk and oil until warm (110°F); then add to flour mixture. Beat on medium speed until dough is stretchy (about 2 minutes). Stir in 1½ cups more flour. Knead dough on a lightly floured board, adding as little remaining flour as necessary to prevent sticking, until smooth and satiny (10 to 15 minutes).

Combine water, 2 tablespoons of the butter, and ¼ cup of the brown sugar; divide equally among 12 muffin cups (2½-inch size). Distribute ½ cup of the pecans equally on top of syrup mixture. Set aside.

On a lightly floured board, roll dough into a 12- by 15-inch rectangle. Brush with remaining butter; top with remaining ¼ cup brown sugar, cinnamon, and remaining ½ cup pecans.

Starting with shorter side, roll rectangle into a tight cylinder; pinch seam to seal. Cut crosswise into twelve 1-inch slices; place each slice in a muffin cup over syrup mixture. Cover rolls and let rise in a warm place until doubled (about 1½ hours).

Bake, uncovered, in a 350° oven until golden brown (20 to 25 minutes). Turn rolls out of pan and serve warm. Makes 12 rolls.

Per roll: 290 calories, 4 g protein, 36 g carbohydrates, 15 g total fat, 14 mg cholesterol, 185 mg sodium

SWEET ENDINGS

Traditional Southwestern desserts are sweet and satisfying, often reflecting the region's Indian and Mexican heritage. There are rich cookies, sturdy puddings full of fruits and nuts, and fried treats such as Buñuelos and Sopaipillas (page 82)—simply dusted with cinnamon sugar or drizzled with honey. The Southwest's Spanish settlers have had an influence too, introducing popular baked flans and a number of other creamy treats.

Though substantial desserts are continuing favorites, the focus today has shifted to lighter fare. Fresh tropical fruits as well as baked fruits appear more frequently. And there's also a growing interest in cool, low-calorie ices, made with or without milk or cream, that provide a refreshing contrast to spicy-hot main dishes. Here we suggest three—pumpkin, pomegranate, and pecan or almond.

BUÑUELOS

Preparation time: About 1 hour
Frying time: About 30 minutes

These large, puffy pastries are made from an egg-rich dough that's crisply fried, then coated with cinnamon sugar. You can make them ahead, if you like, then reheat just before serving.

    4 eggs
   1¼ cups sugar
        About 2 cups all-purpose flour
    1 teaspoon *each* baking powder and salt
        Salad oil
    1 teaspoon ground cinnamon

In large bowl of an electric mixer, beat eggs and ¼ cup of the sugar until thick and lemon-colored. Stir together 1½ cups of the flour, baking powder, and salt; gradually add to egg mixture, beating until well blended. Stir in ¼ cup more flour.

Turn dough out onto a lightly floured board; knead gently, working in as little flour as necessary, until dough is smooth and no longer sticky (about 5 minutes).

Divide dough into 16 equal pieces. With floured hands, shape each piece into a ball. Cover balls with plastic wrap as they are formed and let rest for 20 to 25 minutes. On a floured board, roll each ball into a 5-inch circle; stack circles, separating them with wax paper.

In a wide frying pan, heat 1½ inches oil to 350°F on a deep-frying thermometer. Meanwhile, combine remaining 1 cup sugar and cinnamon and sprinkle into a 9-inch round cake pan. Using tongs, push 1 circle of dough into hot oil and cook, turning once, until golden brown (about 1½ minutes). Remove from oil, drain briefly, place in sugar mixture, and turn to coat thoroughly.

Repeat until all buñuelos are cooked; reserve any leftover sugar mixture. Serve buñuelos warm, sprinkling with reserved sugar mixture, if you like. Or let cool completely and store airtight at room temperature for up to 3 days (freeze for longer storage; thaw unwrapped).

To recrisp, arrange cooled or thawed buñuelos in double layers in shallow baking pans. Bake, uncovered, in a 350° oven until hot (6 to 8 minutes); sprinkle with reserved sugar mixture. Serve warm or cooled. Makes 16 buñuelos.

Per buñuelo: 167 calories, 3 g protein, 28 g carbohydrates, 5 g total fat, 69 mg cholesterol, 182 mg sodium

SPICED CARAMEL CUSTARD FLAN

Preparation time: About 15 minutes
Baking time: About 15 minutes
Chilling time: 6 hours or until next day

Preheating the milk for this golden baked custard intensifies its spicy flavor and shortens the baking time.

    4 whole cloves
    2 *each* whole allspice and cardamom pods, crushed
    1 cinnamon stick (about 2 inches long), broken in half
    2 cups milk
    1 teaspoon vanilla
    ⅔ cup sugar
    6 eggs

In a cheesecloth bag or a tea ball, combine cloves, allspice, cardamom, and cinnamon stick. Place in a 2-quart pan with milk and vanilla; set aside.

In a small frying pan, melt ⅓ cup of the sugar over medium heat, shaking and tilting pan until sugar is caramelized. Immediately pour syrup into a 9-inch pie pan at least 1½ inches deep. Using hot pads, tilt pan quickly so syrup flows over bottom and slightly up sides. If syrup hardens before you finish, set pan over medium heat to soften.

Heat milk and spices over medium heat until steaming hot, then remove from heat and let cool slightly; remove spices. Meanwhile, in a large bowl, beat eggs with remaining ⅓ cup sugar; gradually add heated milk, stirring quickly with a fork.

Set caramel-lined pan in a larger pan and pour in egg mixture. Add enough boiling water to larger pan so it just comes up around edges of pie pan.

Bake in a 350° oven until a ⅜-inch-deep crevice forms when you gently push center of custard with back of a spoon (about 15 minutes).

Remove flan from hot water and refrigerate immediately for at least 6 hours or until next day.

To serve, loosen edge of flan with a knife, then cover pan with a rimmed plate. Holding both together, quickly invert. To serve, cut into wedges and spoon caramel sauce on top. Makes 6 to 8 servings.

Per serving: 163 calories, 7 g protein, 20 g carbohydrates, 6 g total fat, 214 mg cholesterol, 82 mg sodium

POMEGRANATE ICE

Pictured on facing page

Preparation time: 40 to 45 minutes
Chilling time: 12 to 14 hours total

Our colorful ices are perfect desserts for the holiday season. Stored in the freezer, all three stay fresh-tasting for up to a month.

8 to 10 large **pomegranates**
1½ teaspoons grated **lemon peel**
3 to 4 tablespoons **lemon juice**
¾ cup **sugar**

Remove seeds from pomegranates; you need 8 cups seeds. Whirl seeds in a food processor or blender, 1½ to 2 cups at a time, until smooth. Pour puréed seeds through a cheesecloth-lined wire strainer set over a bowl. Let drain; save juice and discard residue. You need 4 cups juice. Stir lemon peel, lemon juice, and sugar into juice until sugar is dissolved. Pour mixture into a 9-inch square metal pan; cover and freeze until solid (at least 8 hours).

Remove ice from freezer; let stand until you can break it into chunks. In a food processor, whirl chunks, about ⅓ at a time; use on-off bursts at first to break up ice, then whirl continuously until mixture is a smooth slush. (Or place all ice in a bowl; break up, then beat with an electric mixer until smooth.)

Return ice to metal pan, cover, and freeze until firm (4 to 6 hours). Let stand at room temperature until slightly softened (about 10 minutes) before serving. Makes 5 cups.

Per ½ cup: 154 calories, 2 g protein, 39 g carbohydrates, .5 g total fat, 0 mg cholesterol, 6 mg sodium

CREAMY PECAN OR ALMOND ICE

Stir together 1½ cups **half-and-half** or milk, ⅓ cup **sugar,** and ½ teaspoon **ground cinnamon** until sugar is dissolved (cinnamon will float). Stir in 1½ cups more **half-and-half** or milk. Freeze and whirl as directed for **Pomegranate Ice,** mixing in 1½ cups coarsely chopped **pecans** or toasted slivered almonds before refreezing. Makes 5 cups.

PUMPKIN ICE

Stir together 1 cup **half-and-half** or milk and ⅔ cup firmly packed **brown sugar** until sugar is dissolved. Then blend in 1 can (16 oz.) **solid-pack pumpkin,** 1½ teaspoons **ground cinnamon,** 1 teaspoon **vanilla,** ½ teaspoon *each* **salt** and **ground ginger,** and ¼ teaspoon *each* **ground cloves** and **ground nutmeg.** Blend in 1¾ cups **half-and-half** or milk. Freeze and whirl as directed for **Pomegranate Ice.** When whirling frozen ice, slowly add enough **half-and-half** or milk (about ¾ cup) to make mixture creamy smooth. Increase standing time before serving to 25 minutes. Makes about 6 cups.

BIZCOCHITOS

Pictured on facing page

Preparation time: About 30 minutes
Baking time: 8 to 12 minutes

In New Mexico, special occasions call for these anise-flavored cookies. Bizcochitos are traditionally made with lard, but you may prefer the flavor of butter.

1 tablespoon **anise seeds**
1 cup **lard** or **butter**
¾ cup **sugar**
1 **egg**
3 cups **all-purpose flour**
1½ teaspoons **baking powder**
½ teaspoon **salt**
3 to 4 tablespoons **brandy** or **dry sherry**
2 teaspoons **ground cinnamon**

Finely crush anise seeds and set aside. In large bowl of an electric mixer, beat lard until creamy; gradually beat in ½ cup of the sugar until sugar granules are dissolved. Then beat in egg.

In another large bowl, mix flour, baking powder, salt, and anise seeds. Gradually beat flour mixture into creamed mixture, alternating with 3 tablespoons of the brandy. Turn out onto a lightly floured board and knead until smooth and pliable (but not sticky), adding a little more brandy, if needed.

Divide dough in half. On a lightly floured board, roll out 1 portion at a time to a ³⁄₁₆-inch-thick rectangle; keep remaining dough covered. Trim edges to straighten sides; add scraps to remaining dough. With a sharp knife, cut dough into 1½- to 2-inch squares. Cut from corners of each square to within ¼ inch of center; grasp corner points on opposite sides, then pinch and push them toward center. (Or cut with small cookie cutters, if you prefer.)

Place cookies slightly apart on ungreased baking sheets. Mix remaining ¼ cup sugar and cinnamon; evenly sprinkle over cookies. Bake in a 350° oven until lightly browned (8 to 12 minutes). Let cool on racks, then store airtight. Makes 4 to 5 dozen cookies.

Per cookie: 65 calories, 1 g protein, 7 g carbohydrates, 4 g total fat, 8 mg cholesterol, 30 mg sodium

For a light ending to an autumn feast, serve velvety Pomegranate Ice (top left)—or our pumpkin- and nut-flavored variations (bottom and top right). Pass Bizcochitos for those who enjoy a cookie on the side. Recipes are on the facing page.

PIÑON FINGERS

Preparation time: About 20 minutes
Baking time: 25 to 30 minutes

While these pine nut cookies are hot from the oven, generously sift powdered sugar over them so it sticks. Then let them cool completely before sampling.

>   1 cup (½ lb.) butter or margarine, at room temperature
> 2¼ cups powdered sugar
>   2 teaspoons vanilla
>   2 cups all-purpose flour
>   1 cup pine nuts

In a large bowl, beat butter, ¼ cup of the sugar, and vanilla until well combined. Stir in flour and pine nuts. Pinch dough into about 2-tablespoon portions; on a lightly floured board, roll each portion into a rope ½ inch thick. Cut rope into 2-inch lengths.

Place pieces of dough, side by side, about 1 inch apart on ungreased 10- by 15-inch baking sheets. Bake in a 275° oven until edges are tinged light golden brown (25 to 30 minutes). Switch baking sheet positions halfway through baking.

While cookies are still warm and on baking sheets, evenly sift remaining 2 cups sugar over them; let cool. Serve, or store airtight at room temperature for up to 1 week (freeze for longer storage). Makes 5 to 6 dozen cookies.

Per cookie: 60 calories, 1 g protein, 7 g carbohydrates, 4 g total fat, 7 mg cholesterol, 26 mg sodium

PASTELITOS

Preparation time: 30 to 40 minutes
Baking time: 12 to 15 minutes

Pastelitos—flaky pastry rectangles with a spiced fruit filling—are one traditional New Mexican holiday dessert. They can be made ahead, ready for festive entertaining.

>   3 cups dried apricots (or 1½ cups dried apricots or pitted prunes and 1½ cups dried apples)
>   ¾ to 1 cup sugar
>   ½ cup water
>   1 tablespoon lemon juice
>   ½ teaspoon ground nutmeg or 1 teaspoon ground cinnamon
>   Flaky Pastry (recipe follows)

Using a food processor or a food chopper fitted with a medium blade, grind dried fruit. Turn fruit into a 2- to 3-quart pan; add sugar, water, lemon juice, and nutmeg. Cook over medium heat, stirring, until mixture boils and becomes very thick (5 minutes). Let cool.

Prepare pastry. On a lightly floured baking sheet, roll out half the dough ⅛ inch thick. Trim edges to make an 8- by 12-inch rectangle; add scraps to remaining dough. Spread fruit mixture over dough to within ⅛ inch of edges. On a lightly floured board, roll out remaining dough and trim to make another 8- by 12-inch rectangle. Place it on top of fruit filling, easing it to fit over other rectangle and pressing it gently onto filling. Prick top. Bake in a 450° oven until lightly browned (12 to 15 minutes).

Let cool; trim edges if overly browned, then cut into about 1½- by 3-inch rectangles. Serve, or store airtight at room temperature for up to 1 week (freeze for longer storage). Makes about 20 fruit bars.

FLAKY PASTRY. Stir together 2 cups **all-purpose flour**, 1 tablespoon **sugar**, 1 teaspoon **baking powder,** and ½ teaspoon **salt.** With a pastry blender, cut in ⅔ cup **solid vegetable shortening** until mixture is crumbly. Add 6 to 7 tablespoons **milk**, a few tablespoons at a time, and mix until evenly moistened. Shape dough into a ball and knead until it holds together.

Per bar: 197 calories, 2 g protein, 32 g carbohydrates, 7 g total fat, 1 mg cholesterol, 81 mg sodium

LAS CRUCES BREAD PUDDING

Preparation time: About 20 minutes
Baking time: About 35 minutes

Bread pudding is a longtime favorite throughout the Southwest. This version is particularly noteworthy—chock-full of cheese, raisins, and nuts.

>   1 cup firmly packed brown sugar
>   1 cup water
>   1 cinnamon stick (3 inches long)
>   ½ loaf (1-lb. size) French bread
>   ½ cup *each* toasted pine nuts, toasted slivered almonds, and chopped pecans
>   1 cup raisins
>   8 ounces jack cheese, cut into ½-inch cubes
>   1 tart apple, thinly sliced
>   Vanilla ice cream or whipped cream

In a 2-quart pan, boil sugar, water, and cinnamon stick until slightly thickened (about 5 minutes). Discard cinnamon stick; set syrup aside.

Cut bread into ½-inch-thick slices. Toast slices, then break into large pieces. Place half the bread in a greased 9- by 13-inch baking dish. Top evenly with half the pine nuts, then with half the almonds, pecans, raisins, and cheese. Top with all the apple slices. Pour half the cinnamon syrup over all. Repeat layers and top with remaining syrup. Bake, covered, in a 350° oven until heated through (about 35 minutes; remove cover for last 5 minutes). Serve warm. To reheat, bake, covered, in a 350° oven for about 15 minutes.

To serve, spoon into individual dishes and top with vanilla ice cream. Makes 8 to 10 servings.

Per serving: 402 calories, 12 g protein, 51 g carbohydrates, 19 g total fat, 21 mg cholesterol, 263 mg sodium

MANGO CREAM

Preparation time: About 15 minutes
Chilling time: 2 to 4 hours

The mango's flavor is peachlike, its aroma flowery. Use fresh or canned fruit in this luscious blend of whipped cream, mangoes, oranges, and nuts.

---

  5 **large ripe mangoes; or 2 cans**
      (14 oz. *each*) mangoes, drained
      Sugar
  2 **large oranges, peeled, seeded, and cut**
      into small pieces
  1 **tablespoon lemon juice**
  2 **cups whipping cream**
  1 **cup pecan pieces**
 12 **pecan halves**

Peel fresh mangoes; cut fruit off pits. Whirl fresh or canned mangoes in a blender until smooth. Add sugar to taste. Stir in oranges and lemon juice. Whip cream until it holds peaks, then fold into mango mixture with pecan pieces. Spoon into individual stemmed glasses and refrigerate for 2 to 4 hours. Garnish with pecan halves before serving. Makes 12 servings.

Per serving: 252 calories, 2 g protein, 21 g carbohydrates, 19 g total fat, 44 mg cholesterol, 16 mg sodium

SOUR CREAM–TOPPED PINEAPPLE

Preparation time: 10 to 15 minutes

Fresh-cut pineapple chunks, mounded in pineapple shells, are crowned with a creamy sauce, nuts, and coconut—a refreshing finale after a spicy entrée.

  1 **large pineapple (about 4½ lbs.)**
 ⅔ **cup sour cream**
  1 **tablespoon firmly packed brown sugar**
 ⅓ **cup chopped pecans or salted peanuts**
 ⅓ **cup sweetened shredded coconut**

Cut pineapple in half lengthwise through crown, then use a grapefruit knife to cut away fruit ½ inch from shells. Lift out fruit, remove core, cut fruit into bite-size pieces, and return to shells.

Mix sour cream and sugar; spoon over pineapple. Just before serving, sprinkle with nuts and coconut. Makes about 6 servings.

Per serving: 209 calories, 2 g protein, 28 g carbohydrates, 11 g total fat, 11 mg cholesterol, 27 mg sodium

BAKED APPLES WITH COWBOY CREAM

Pictured on page 94

Preparation time: About 15 minutes
Baking time: 20 to 30 minutes

This simple dessert resembles a crustless apple pie. Fragile Buñuelos (page 89) can be offered as a pastry accompaniment.

---

  4 **medium-size Golden Delicious or**
      Rome Beauty apples (or 2 of each)
 ¼ **cup butter or margarine, melted**
 ¼ **cup firmly packed brown sugar**
 ¼ **cup coffee-flavored liqueur**
      Cowboy Cream (recipe follows)
      Ground cinnamon

Core apples, then cut into ⅛- to ¼-inch-thick wedges. Overlap wedges in a buttered shallow 9- to 10-inch round baking dish. Pour butter over top; sprinkle with sugar and liqueur.

Bake, uncovered, in a 350° oven until apples are tender when pierced (20 to 30 minutes).

Prepare Cowboy Cream; cover and refrigerate.

Serve apples warm or at room temperature, topped with Cowboy Cream and sprinkled with cinnamon. Makes 6 to 8 servings.

COWBOY CREAM. In a bowl, combine 1 cup **whipping cream,** 1 tablespoon *each* **powdered sugar** and **coffee-flavored liqueur,** and ¼ teaspoon **ground cinnamon.** Whip until cream holds peaks. Cover and refrigerate for up to 4 hours.

Per serving: 222 calories, 1 g protein, 22 g carbohydrates, 15 g total fat, 49 mg cholesterol, 71 mg sodium

Baked Apples with Cowboy Cream (recipe on page 93) can be served warm or at room temperature. For an attractive presentation, arrange wedges of baked red and golden apples in a swirl; then add a puff of coffee-flavored whipped cream.